# The

6

# Pillars of Civility

# *The* 6

## *Pillars of Civility*

Living a balanced life in a chaotic world
through the powers of awareness,
compassion, humility, gratitude,
encouragement and responsibility.

## Jay Remer

# The 6 Pillars of Civility

Living a balanced life in a chaotic world
through the powers of awareness, compassion, humility,
gratitude, encouragement and responsibility.

Inquiries:
Winds Are Inn Inc.
132 Water Street, Saint Andrews, NB, Canada E5B 1A8
Contact: John H. Remer, Jr
Email: jay@etiquetteguy.com

Production Management:
Robyn M Fritz MA MBA CHt, Alchemy West

Copyediting:
Laurel Robinson, Laurel Robinson Editorial Services

Layout:
Robert Lanphear, Lanphear Design

Design:
Greg Cohane, Gregory P. Cohane Design

Print ISBN: 978-1-7778711-0-9
E-Book ISBN: 978-1-7778711-1-6

# Contents

## *Pillar 6 —* **RESPONSIBILITY**

# Foreword

In our time-poor world, people often forget to stop, step back, and think about their actions and the consequences to others. Part of the deal in life is interacting with other people. We do this daily, and yet so many people get it wrong. Either intentionally or unintentionally, we can damage our relationships with others with alarming ease. We must get our relationships right to navigate our passage through the winding journey of life with merit and aplomb.

Jay Remer, The Etiquette Guy, understands this. It becomes obvious from the first paragraph in this impressive work.

Many of the successful titles on etiquette and manners deal with the facts, which is always helpful; however, most do not back them up with the reasons why.

This book goes deeper. Without any pretense, it looks at human behaviour and presents sound arguments for easy decorum and mannerly living, outlining the logic and merits of being nice to one another—something which is always needed, but especially today.

Jay Remer's essays, jottings, and musings on his subject offer a considered take on civility, presented in the six pillars metaphor. Civility is at the core of what Jay believes and preaches in his renowned workshops, seminars, and writings.

If more people would emulate the generosity, gentleness, compassion, and loyalty to the human spirit shown here and by Jay in his private and professional life, the world would be much richer.

I challenge anyone in their right mind to disagree with the underlying message of what follows.

**William Hanson**
British etiquette coach and author
London, April 2021

# *Introduction*

The six pillars of civility are the building blocks of decent human behavior. More than ever before, we need a road map to civility. So many people seem lost and overwhelmed, and there is an appetite for returning to a society where we treat each other with respect and courtesy. How did we devolve to the divisive, unjust, and fearful state too many of us now endure? After all, life has been pretty good for most of us, especially compared with the suffering of so many people worldwide. Yet, we seem to have slipped into an abyss where we have lost our shared humanity.

Fortunately, thanks to a handful of curious scientists, we are beginning to understand how our brains function, which allows us to realize that our behaviors are primarily grounded in keeping us alive, not in making us happy. We now know that trauma, especially childhood trauma, influences how we respond and behave throughout our lives. We are also learning how to heal from our traumas and live the fulfilling lives we deserve. Unfortunately, the professional assistance we need to help us heal is woefully inadequate, so we are on our own to try to patch our lives back together as best we can.

I wrote this book to understand better how the six pillars of civility—awareness, compassion, humility, gratitude, compassion, encouragement, and responsibility—resonate with us and how we can more easily incorporate them into our daily lives.

These short essays offer a glimpse into my personal experience in regaining balance in my own life. I am fortunate to have had many guides along the way who shared their life experiences with me as illustrations of their healing process. Others served as professional counselors and mentors. Without their presence and steadfast determination, I would be unable to write this. You, too, must uncover and heal from your traumas. Ideally, this book will illuminate some new perspectives on how to behave and focus your attention as you follow your path.

Although these essays may not teach specific skills, they can help raise civility to a level where we treat others with respect as equals. We should all recognize fundamental human rights. In the United States and Canada, most of us have been denied these rights because of the power and control model of governance we have regrettably elected. It's our responsibility as citizens to elect more responsive governments that will enable us to live in a more inclusive, respectful, and decent world.

In the context of this book, I define civility as how people interact with one another with mutual respect and kindness both publicly and in their private interactions. Civility is the umbrella under which etiquette and decorum rest. Because we are surrounded by overwhelming incivility, I thought sharing my observations could offer a positive perspective on how to regain civility, often by employing the self-reflective exercises that follow each chapter.

The words I chose to identify different aspects of civility came to me through self-reflection, meditation, and discussions with peers. In the years of answering thousands of questions about etiquette and human dynamics, I haven't found any question that can't be answered within one or more of these aspects.

Because this is not an attempt to discuss the topic with scholarly references and anecdotes beyond my own life experience, this pick-up, put-down book can provide anyone looking for answers to a variety of life's challenges an opportunity for inward, quiet reflection.

*Pillar 1*

# AWARENESS

# Introduction

*If, then, I were asked for the most important advice I could
give, that which I considered to be the most useful to the
men of our century, I should simply say: in the name of
God, stop a moment, cease your work, look around you.*

— Leo Tolstoy

L et's begin our exploration of civility with awareness,
which I define as being mindful of the people and things
around us, primarily our effect on one another. If we are to
build healthy lives and sustain vibrant communities, we must
open our eyes. But, unfortunately, in the fast-paced, time-
starved lifestyles many of us choose to lead, awareness seems
to all but disappear. That's a tragedy and a real danger to civi-
lized society, because we often become more reclusive and less
connected to each other.

Our instincts lead us to awaken to the world around us.
Becoming fully engaged opens the doors to a fun, exciting,
and fulfilling life.

Self-awareness is an essential aspect of awareness we cannot afford to ignore. How often can we remember feeling like
we were too busy to acknowledge our friends and family who
reached significant milestones or accomplishments? Unfortu-

nately, none of us are immune to this lack of awareness. We can't be bothered with writing thank-you notes. We even miss birthdays and anniversaries.

This disregard can lead to an erosion of civility and the friendships and connections we desire. A healthy society comprises many interdependent relationships. We cannot thrive without them; we need each other for our very survival. So it stands to reason that awareness is a critical component of our daily lives. Undoubtedly, we would be much happier, feel safer, and have a greater sense of self-worth if we engaged with others more effectively and became more aware of our place in the world. As we make mistakes, meet personal challenges, and strive to succeed and feel safe and secure, greater awareness helps us act with grace, compassion, and humility.

Too often, we drift through life with no real sense of what's happening because we are not fully engaged. Sadly, we miss out on what life has to offer while we endure fear without taking the time to connect with others. Feelings of isolation can develop, and progress and productivity come to a screeching halt. We experienced this during COVID-19, when feelings of loneliness intensified.

Being isolated can also impede our success at work. Teamwork is usually a vital component of a healthy and encouraging business environment. Collaboration requires an ongoing awareness of what our teammates are doing. Without this finely honed skill, everyone suffers.

Awareness brings to mind two familiar phrases: "deer in the headlights" and "stop and smell the roses." How often do we feel like we're caught unaware, and life is rushing by us? When do we take the time to enjoy what we are doing and who we are doing it with, even if it is just with ourselves? Slowing down to allow life to come into focus helps us achieve our goals, whatever they may be, from a happy family to a successful career. Even both!

Awareness of what we do, our real intentions for doing it, and how we feel about it helps us interact more gracefully with others. It also leads to respectful relationships, a healthy and productive work environment, and a thriving family.

# The Gift of "Small Spaces"

*The universe buries strange jewels deep within us all and*
*then stands back to see if we can find them. The hunt to*
*uncover those jewels—that's creative living.*

— Elizabeth Gilbert

---

Awareness often appears instantaneously. We find it in the most unlikely places at the most unlikely times. While living in a vast universe, we can uncover surprising insights in the smallest of spaces.

Ideas such as awareness, compassion, and civility have become part of everyday conversation for adults and children. With today's emphasis on addressing and eradicating incivility and bullying, which add unnecessary stress to our lives, such discussions have emerged like so many flowers in a garden. How incredibly refreshing and promising! As Byron Katie asserts, "No one is too young or too old to have their feelings hurt, to be confused, or frustrated, or depressed. And everyone deserves to know how to deal with their suffering."

For many of us, growing up meant dealing with these same dynamics but with a sparse set of tools and an emotional denial mindset. Let's face it: rarely does anyone have a perfect childhood. We were told to "just get over it" or heard "sorry about your luck" or "life isn't fair." Today, I find these dismissive instructions as useless and cruel as when I was a child. Because we don't understand what handling stressful situations involves, many of us are still grappling with the same struggles we experienced as children. The coping mechanisms we have adopted to survive have created stressful lives filled with insecurity, low self-esteem, and incivility. What can we do to improve how we handle stress in our lives?

We can reduce stress by breaking down stressful thoughts into manageable pieces: we can more easily see the total picture by examining the parts that create it. Only by looking at overwhelming situations or feelings as individual pieces of the whole can we begin to cope with what is going on.

Where to begin is the biggest challenge for most of us, because taking the first step can be scary. Having no clear path often stops us from beginning at all. The best way to move forward is to break our actions down into smaller steps. Much to my surprise, when I started taking small steps, I discovered hidden gems of information. I refer affectionately to these little gems as "the good stuff," and where they live is what I refer to as "the small spaces."

The small spaces exist between breaths, thoughts, or lines in a book. We usually don't think about these small spaces, but we can uncover the little gems that comfort us when we take the time to do so. We then remember just how much we miss as we glide through life. It is in these small spaces where civility hangs its hat. They are also where common sense begins, and we discover, through trial and error, what works and what doesn't.

To discover this for yourself, you will need to commit some time to this practice. One of the discoveries I made on my journey is how little "free" time I thought I had. The commitment I made to myself included permitting myself to set aside "me" time. Initially this seemed quite selfish. However, I quickly realized how important it was to set aside "me" time each day. If we sit quietly, we let our minds open to reveal our most profound inner feelings and thoughts without being distracted by our tasks. By listening quietly, we can gain valuable insight into our suffering. We can discover ways to reduce unnecessary stress and eventually eliminate it. It's an exercise that provides enormous benefits with relatively little effort. It only needs to take a few minutes a day. Try it: make "me" time a priority.

# Please Push My Wheelchair

*The purpose of life is not to be happy. It is to be useful, to be honorable, to be compassionate, to have it make some difference that you have lived and lived well.*

— Ralph Waldo Emerson

I once spoke about civility at a launch for a book about bullying in the workplace. The guests were an eclectic mix of friends who had traveled from as far away as California to support the author, Andrew Faas. Several speakers shared their experiences about bullying at work and about initiatives underway to bring greater awareness to this serious and complex issue and announce new actions to make some fundamental changes.

One of the most interesting people I met that evening was a journalist in a wheelchair. She asked me for my business card as I stood beside her during a brief pause. She had listened to my remarks about the six pillars of civility, which align with the underlying dynamics of Faas' book. She writes about human atrocities, past and present. The fact that my words resonated with her meant a great deal to me. I felt a rush of gratitude.

Later I went to speak with her again. I had left my business cards in my car 150 miles away, so I wanted to write down and exchange contact information with her. She smiled when she learned I was Canada's Etiquette Guy and wrote columns about etiquette and civility, and she asked me to read the sign on the back of her wheelchair. Most placards I had seen on wheelchairs in New York were pleas for money or food. This sign simply said, "Please Push My Wheelchair." Frankly, I thought it was an unusual request. Without prompting, she related to me why she carried the sign: it provided clarification and allowed people to assist her and others who might need a push.

As I pondered her message, I knew there was more to this simple request than meets the eye. She went on to explain how important it is to give people opportunities to help each other.

I had never properly considered this perspective before, but it made perfect sense. Connecting with others is the most natural and important action we engage in throughout our life. It follows that being of service is an essential ingredient in maintaining healthy communities. Something as simple as giving someone a gentle push, especially when they are facing an uphill challenge, can be of paramount importance.

Being aware of those around us who need assistance allows us to connect on a fundamental level. As community members, we have a responsibility to be part of the process of transforming our weakest links into pillars of strength. Coincidentally, it is very satisfying to lend a helping hand or receive a gentle push.

Finally, when we metaphorically push a wheelchair, we encourage that person to continue on their path, realizing that we cannot always succeed alone. We become comfortable knowing that connecting in this way is not a sign of weakness but of strength and cooperation. In many of the activities we engage in throughout the day, we need to establish connections and work in concert with our friends, family, and coworkers.

The next time you see someone who needs their "wheelchair" pushed, stop, ask them if they would like some help, and, if they say yes, take the time to help them. By giving others a push, we enrich our lives and help sustain safe and healthy communities where we can live our lives to the fullest.

# Through the Eyes of
# the Dining Room Table

*It has been said, "time heals all wounds." I do not agree.
The wounds remain. In time, the mind, protecting its sanity,
covers them with scar tissue and the pain lessens.
But it is never gone.*

— Rose Fitzgerald Kennedy

A s he slid open the barn door, the antiques dealer ushered my newlywed parents into his workshop filled with cobwebs and piles of "old wood furniture." A table covered in half-empty paint cans caught my mother's eye. The dealer explained that it would need some work, but it had gorgeous legs and the proportions were perfect for the dining room. Being a determined woman, my mother persuaded the cabinetmaker to do his best to restore the table to its former glory.

Over the years, the table hosted many dinner parties and was where my sister and I learned to eat once we outgrew eating with our hands. The table's beautiful dark mahogany surface sparkled. We used place mats instead of a tablecloth, and the sound of placing knives and forks and spoons every day has left an indelible mark on me. There was never any noisy clanking; it had a measured, purposeful tone, much like the way good conversations flow.

Like the conversation, which remained civil, yet uninteresting, the table was rarely fully expanded. But when we added the large leaves and set the table for a formal dinner, the conversations developed into more meaningful exchanges of ideas. Here we learned real lessons. We discovered different foods and how to eat them correctly; we became aware of where they were grown and who produced them. We explored animal husbandry and discussed hunting and shooting. We learned that food originates in wild, natural settings, not on grocery store shelves. Understanding these concepts helped create images in my mind's eye. As a result, I realized that I relate more successfully with the world through pictures than words.

We learned to discuss politics and economics at an early age. We became aware of and learned to appreciate the strengths of people elected to office and spent far less time discussing their weaknesses. Leading politicians, great athletes, and a few entertainers became our mentors. The dining table was a haven, a brief respite from the challenges of growing up in the combat zone of a privileged but highly dysfunctional family.

I learned how to serve and clear the table, making sure not to drop anything as I moved silently around the room. This skill came quickly, and I enjoyed it. I am grateful that the table witnessed and experienced my newly acquired abilities.

My sister and I usually ate early and together at the large table. There we would discuss our day at school, how we would avoid our mother's quirky behavior, and how relieved we would feel when our father would come home. He was our only hope for protection from our brutal, dictatorial, and oppressive mother.

We grew up at that table. We became adolescents, and then one day, that table was gone. Through the ravages of life, divorces, new houses, and blended families, the table needed to find a new home. A museum benefited from its departure. It was sold as an original Duncan Phyfe, which it was, and is now gracing another lucky family's dining room. It will never forget what it heard while in our care, as it did in the care of countless previous families, even while resting under the paint cans and cobwebs.

I hope it retains the peace and comfort it afforded us as children. After all, dining room tables overhear some of the most meaningful conversations families have.

# Sidewalk Etiquette

*I only went out for a walk and finally concluded to stay out*
*till sundown, for going out, I found, was going in.*

— John Muir

⌒

One of life's simple pleasures is strolling along a city side-walk, enjoying a bit of window-shopping. Gliding past brightly decorated storefronts transports us far away from the hustle and bustle of our everyday lives and into a gentler, quieter space. We allow our thoughts to drift in different directions.

We use sidewalks as safe paths to travel on foot around town. They keep us away from cars and trucks and usually safe from bicycles, skateboards, and roller skates. After a heavy rain, sidewalks protect us from puddles and oil-slicked roadways.

Sidewalks are for pedestrian traffic, and sharing them comfortably requires observing a few simple, polite rules. As an example, for some reason, on the busiest of days, families decide to gleefully stroll down the sidewalk side by side, oblivious of others, and preventing fellow pedestrians from passing in either direction. When the eventual collision appears imminent, the family rarely closes ranks or even steps to one side. Is this rudeness because of a sense of entitlement or obliviousness?

No matter how you look at sidewalk traffic, we all need to be more aware of other people sharing the same path. Awareness requires looking around and seeing who is nearby: Are they going in our direction or against us? Are they in a hurry and carrying bags, or are they guiding small children? To avoid creating sidewalk missteps, take a moment to look around and be aware of your surroundings. Treat sidewalks as roads: walk and pass in the same direction as traffic does. Sidewalks would then be safer and more enjoyable.

# Shopping with Humility

*Anyone who believes the competitive spirit in America is dead has never been in a supermarket when the cashier opens another checkout line.*

— Ann Landers

Navigating the aisles of a store can be fraught with challenges. Many shoppers are in a terrible rush, stressed out, and accompanied by excited children who are impatient and needy. Increasingly narrow aisles, larger shopping carts, and an ever-growing choice of products add to this confusion.

Don't block the aisle with your shopping cart. Especially on the busier weekend days, being aware of the space you and your cart are occupying helps avoid collisions. Although this seems like common sense, many people fail to move their carts out of the way. Sometimes this is unavoidable. In such cases, I recommend the 10-second rule. If you need more than 10 seconds to find what you need, move your cart out of the way and continue your hunt unencumbered.

Keep track of your children. Understandably, little ones delight in running up and down the aisles where their favorite treats await. Although it is a good idea to teach children how to shop and where to find things in the store, it is helpful to remember that this is neither a playground nor a day care center. Unruly children are annoying and hazardous, especially if other shoppers can't see them over their carts. Keep free-range children under your watchful eye at all times.

Talking on cell phones, especially while interacting with store employees, is rude and disrespectful to those on the phone as well as to the person in front of you. This disrespect is a form of bullying and sets a poor example for children. Cell phones come in very handy when shopping, allowing you to plan meals or compare prices. However, conversations should be private, discreet, and out of earshot.

Don't just abandon your shopping cart in the parking lot. There are designated areas for returning carts: use them. Being inconsiderate is lazy, and leaving your cart creates an obstacle for others trying to park. Put yourself in the next shopper's shoes. They will appreciate it.

Don't criticize employees for store deficiencies. Berating anyone in a public setting is unacceptable and will not solve a thing. If you have a legitimate complaint, discuss it privately with the store manager. The stock person is not responsible for limp vegetables, relocated items, or any other problem. Managers know how to handle customer service issues responsibly.

Don't have a heated discussion or argue with other customers or, worse yet, with your children. Remember, supermarket aisles are public spaces, not places to fight or bring attention to yourself inappropriately. Other shoppers find this behavior unsettling. If you must have a confrontation, do so in private. After all, many professionals agree that yelling at a child is as abusive as hitting a child.

These are just some of the actions that influence any shopping experience. We've all witnessed them. Many of us can even remember being guilty of them. Let's remember to make shopping a pleasant experience. Everyone benefits. Even when we are in a terrible hurry, we cannot forget to take the time to be civil.

# Moving from Fear to Calm

*Only when we are no longer afraid do we begin to live.*

— Dorothy Thompson

⌐◡⌐

I had the privilege of teaching a group of immigrants who were aspiring entrepreneurs. As part of the Business Immigrant Mentoring Program, the participants had plenty of questions about understanding Canada's business culture. Surprisingly, most of the queries from these budding entrepreneurs were similar to those posed by non-immigrants. The two most prevalent themes were learning to communicate effectively and making connections to further their businesses. What also came to light as the most challenging obstacle to success was the fear of making mistakes.

This same fear is prevalent in many workplaces. Two studies conducted by the Faas Foundation in partnership with Mental Health America and the Yale Center for Emotional Intelligence showed that over 70 percent of workers find their jobs unfulfilling, do not speak highly of their bosses, and are looking for other jobs. Sadly, this dynamic produces a culture of fear where bullying and unnecessary stress are the underlying reasons for 120,000 deaths per year caused by stress at work. Also, the loss of productivity translates to a $1.5 trillion loss to the North American economy annually. These statistics are significant, and we must take them seriously if we are to return civility and success to the workplace.

How do we move from a culture of fear to one where the workplace is psychologically safe, healthy, and fair? This shift requires a conscious effort by all concerned to want to see a change. Enough people must want to embrace the ethic of reciprocity (the Golden Rule) and employ common sense.

The path to creating a cultural revolution always begins with each of us as individuals. We are reminded of this every time a flight attendant directs us to first put our own oxygen mask on before assisting others. This directive mirrors how life works in general. We must be sure to have our own house in order before we can effectively be of any assistance.

How to do that? Consider the breath. Perhaps I am a slow learner. Or maybe I am stubborn and committed to a resistance to change, but I have ignored the importance of the breath until recently. Although we need to breathe to stay alive, we can change our world from fear to calm when we purposefully use this automatic function.

We have all heard the directive to just calm down. That is one of those friendly suggestions that often fall on deaf ears because we have no idea how to accomplish this! Intentional breathing is one easy and successful answer. Try this the next time you are feeling stressed. Take four nice, long, even breaths, and you'll find that a feeling of calm begins to replace the stress. Then you can start to process rational thoughts and figure stuff out again.

Once you have regained balance and feel centered, encourage others within your circle to do the same. A calm state of mind allows us to respect others and listen to what they have to say.

This change of behavior is also proving useful in schools and organizations. Schools are introducing time-outs in the form of meditation breaks. Many workplaces provide quiet rooms where people can regain their composure after a particularly challenging situation. A calm mind achieves clear thinking. A fearful mind thinks only of surviving the immediate moment. Which way do you prefer?

Take an honest look at your life and ask yourself if you like what you are doing personally and professionally. Then ask yourself why. If you aren't feeling fulfilled or even safe, do you realize that you can change that? Some of us need to change jobs, some of us need to edit our list of friends, or we may decide that seeking professional counselling would be helpful.

These choices are all significant. We need to remember to have compassion for those who are making their lives so challenging. We must also have compassion for ourselves and all human beings. We need to connect with others for our very survival. But the people with whom we connect are our choice.

# Safety and Civility
# Go Hand in Hand

*As economies change, so do communication skills. From*
*these changes, a need arises for new ways to incorporate a*
*healthy social compass into our lives.*

— Cindy Ann Peterson

Feeling safe and secure is a basic human need. We instinctively do whatever we can to move away from things that we fear or cause us pain and toward people or things that protect us or give us pleasure. It is within this sense of security that we form our communities. When events disrupt our feelings of safety, we immediately revert to the fight, flight, or freeze responses designed to keep us alive.

Unfortunately, our brains are complex and not designed to be the smooth-running engines we would like. We regularly bounce back and forth between feeling safe and feeling frightened. Each state of awareness elicits a different response. When we feel secure, we naturally connect with others more readily than when we are frightened. In today's highly stressed existence, most of us continually look over our shoulders, waiting for the next proverbial shoe to drop. This culture of fear is ripping our society to shreds. Many of us feel as though our ship has lost its rudder.

This fear knows no bounds. I haven't met anyone who cannot relate to this state of discomfort. We look around us and see poverty, despair, and frustration. Some of us live with this reality, many turn a blind eye to the pain, and a growing number devote their lives to making a better life for the less fortunate. Every single step that we take toward alleviating suffering helps heal a battered society.

Is this the way we want to live? Is this the world we want to leave to the next generation? Shouldn't everyone have the chance to live a fulfilling, abundant life?

Feeling safe and secure is the keystone of civility. Only when we are not on constant guard can we exhale and enjoy a more thoughtful and purposeful life. This dynamic is in play throughout our lives, beginning at birth, if not before. Every opposing force that we encounter impacts the very fabric of our existence. These forces can be emotional and mental as well as physical. Socioeconomic factors influence how much negativity we will face, but only to a degree.

We must understand the incredible amount of time and work it takes to heal the damage created by this negativity. Current thinking is that many of these challenges have overwhelmed the system. Leaders are scrambling to find solutions, all while their constituents or employees continue to be frustrated. Unfortunately, every moment a person suffers, they need more inner courage and outer support to rebalance their life.

Taking personal responsibility for ourselves is how we can most effectively make positive changes in our lives. Knowing what is happening solidifies our foundation, allowing us to better understand where to take our next step.

We aren't going to solve all of our problems magically. Nor can or should we expect the government to do it. But we can improve our happiness by gaining a greater understanding of what we're actually doing. The next time you act out in frustration or anger at your child, partner, coworker, or employee, know that you are inflicting damage, creating fear, and contributing to their suffering.

We are not likely to stop or change our behaviors overnight. Still, with compassion for others and ourselves, we can make a great start. Regaining balance in our lives is not usually a process we can work through without help. Most often, this help comes from friends and family. Professional counseling can accelerate the healing process, help prevent mental illnesses from worsening, and improve our overall mental health. A willingness to seek out and accept this kind of help remains a challenge today because of the harsh stigma around mental illness.

Knowing how important safety is in achieving and maintaining a healthy community, we need to encourage one another to find more balance and less turmoil. Civility should not be a mysterious concept meant only for a chosen few. It is a way of life we all deserve. How will you alleviate suffering and negativity in your life and in the lives of those you love?

# *Self-Reflective Exercises*

With this group of exercises, and those at the end of each chapter, find a quiet place and ask yourself:

- What matters most to you in your life?

- Practice sitting alone and quietly at least once a day. Be aware of your thoughts and let them pass without judgment. Notice any physical sensations. Consider journaling about them.

- Visit the small spaces. Investigate them, allowing them to expand and reveal your inner self.

- What causes stress in your life, and what brings you contentment and fulfillment?

- Write any new glimpses of understanding in a small notebook or journal as often as you can. Going back over these notes helps you strengthen these understandings and create new and healthier patterns.

- Do not censor or judge your thoughts during this quiet time.

# Pillar 2
# COMPASSION

# Introduction

*Love and compassion are necessities, not luxuries. Without them, humanity cannot survive.*

— His Holiness the Dalai Lama

⌒

Compassion and self-compassion are two of life's most important qualities that require continual practice to appreciate fully. As challenging as it can be to have compassion for others, it is usually even more challenging to have self-compassion. Too often, we set unreasonably high standards for ourselves. When we don't reach them, we become disappointed and beat ourselves up. We need to lighten up and give ourselves a break once in a while. We all have challenges and imperfections. If we do not accept this and embrace it, warts and all, we cannot fully appreciate the uniqueness of the folks we meet along the way.

Throughout our lives, we experience disappointments that can leave us feeling unworthy, sad, or depressed. With compassion and humility, we can develop empathy, the ability to sense these feelings in others. We can help them navigate challenging times simply by being present. Although it is not our responsibility to fix other people's problems, we can give great comfort by connecting with them compassionately.

Life provides us with many opportunities to connect with others, and sometimes choosing between one thing and another presents real challenges. For example, if given a choice between going to a wedding or a funeral, which would you choose? Some people would choose to attend the happier wedding, yet our friends need us the most during times of stress. How often are we present for our friends? How often are we present for ourselves?

Having compassion is also essential in our professional lives. We form different relationships at work than we do socially. Although the rules and dynamics may differ, the underlying principles are the same.

A friend once related to me how his life was rapidly unraveling. He had failed in business and felt like he was also failing at home. Although we don't relish this sort of phone call, a friend in need is a friend indeed. Because he was feeling alone and needed a sympathetic ear, I took the time to listen carefully to him. Although I could only commiserate with him, that is most likely what he needed more than anything. He needed to feel that someone could relate to his difficulties. Relieving the feeling of loneliness is a compassionate gesture.

Most of us have experienced professional and personal failures. It is part of the life experience. We must allow ourselves to make mistakes, make apologies, forgive ourselves, move on, and, ideally, avoid repeating the same errors.

Life presents all of us with challenges. Yet rarely are challenges too difficult to handle. But when we do feel overwhelmed, we should be comfortable reaching out to our friends and family for support. Some of us use the excuse that we don't want to be a bother. My advice is to be a bother. We cannot fight all of our battles alone, nor should we.

Having compassion for others and for ourselves allows us to handle our daily challenges and help others with theirs.

# Apology Accepted

*A stiff apology is a second insult. The injured party does
not want to be compensated because he has been wronged;
he wants to be healed because he has been hurt.*

— Gilbert K. Chesterton

L et's face it. We all make mistakes. Most of the time, we
recognize them and take appropriate remedial action,
but sometimes we don't. Some errors are significant, dangerous, and frightening; others are relatively simple and of little
consequence. Apologizing for our mistakes with humility not
only shows that we have compassion for others but is also the
decent, respectful thing to do. Saying "I'm sorry" is something
we should learn to do at an early age. It shows that we understand the difference between right and wrong.

What happens if we don't apologize? Maybe we don't
recognize when we've made a mistake that causes physical,
mental, or emotional harm. Are we unaware of how our words
and actions affect those around us? We may carry on in bliss-
ful ignorance of our misdeed, but eventually the damage will
surface as hurt feelings, grudges, "the silent treatment," or flat-
out anger. Then the need for an apology becomes apparent,
yet because of the passage of time, apologizing becomes more
awkward.

Nonetheless, we cannot overemphasize the importance of this simple, humble act. Without an apology, deep wounds can result, friendships can be in peril, and intense anger can fester. We have all witnessed this, and many of us have felt it first-hand. It is essential to teach this concept at home and school. If we don't learn this skill during childhood, it will be more challenging to understand it later in life.

Being aware of someone else's feelings is an important aspect of our emotional intelligence, so when we unintentionally hurt them, we should learn to quickly adjust our tone and apologize. These are valuable skills we should practice throughout life. Being unaware of or unable to recognize our mistakes displays selfishness and disrespect.

Sometimes saying we are sorry feels like releasing the top from a pressure cooker—it's a time to exhale, smile, and re-establish a close bond. Everyone feels better. The requisite acceptance of the apology completes the circle.

Remembering not to diminish anyone helps make the effort more graceful. When someone apologizes to you, if you feel it is sincere, acknowledge them by forgiving them. Ignoring them will indicate your unwillingness to forgive them.

Forgiveness is an act of kindness that reveals our compassion. It demonstrates our shared humanity, and we feel a sense of safety in this commonality. These are the moments I have often heard referred to as "one day we will look back and laugh about this."

Saying we are sorry has its challenges. Our fragile egos can get the better of us and prioritize the need to be right over doing the right thing.

When we make big mistakes, it takes more courage, humility, and self-compassion to own them and apologize. It reflects the respect we have for other people and, in turn, for ourselves. We need to understand that hurtful acts and harsh words have consequences.

We must handle mistakes appropriately and with compassion. Taking responsibility for the error of our ways is the first step. Making an appropriate apology is the next step, defusing any negative energy the error may have created. Finally, find a solution to rectify the problem. When we make a mistake, it is our responsibility to fix it, not someone else's. With self-compassion, we can more readily accept our responsibility. Be gentle with yourself and with others, and compassion will follow.

# People Living with Disabilities

*Part of the problem with the word "disabilities" is that it immediately suggests an inability to see or hear or walk or do other things that many of us take for granted. But what of people who can't feel? Or talk about their feelings? Or manage their feelings in constructive ways? What of people who aren't able to form close and strong relationships? And people who cannot find fulfillment in their lives, or those who have lost hope, who live in disappointment and bitterness and find in life no joy, no love? These, it seems to me, are the real disabilities.*

— Fred Rogers

S omething to remember about people living with any disability is that they are acutely aware of their situation and adjust to it better than we do. Deciding that someone needs our help and even how to help is usually not our responsibility. If they need our help, they will ask for it in most cases. Interfering may further impede their abilities instead of being helpful.

Someone using a wheelchair is generally not hard of hearing or unable to understand a normal conversation. Yet some people tend to raise their voices and speak more slowly and deliberately to people with evident mobility issues. Speaking this way is insulting and embarrassing and can be awkward. From a compassionate perspective, a person engaging with someone living with a disability should come away from the interaction with greater awareness of just what it's like to live that way.

Servers should never ask anyone accompanying the person with a disability what the person wants to eat or drink. People are perfectly capable of speaking for themselves and making any other decision.

This story shows how assumptions can backfire. A woman using crutches and a friend managed to get two seats at a crowded bar. The only available seats left were right next to them. Two men approached and asked if they could join them. The women were delighted to have the company and welcomed them. Little did the gentlemen know that the two had decided to conduct a social experiment and swap roles for the evening. When the men saw a pair of crutches leaning against the wall and asked who they belonged to, the women explained that Jane, seated closest to the crutches, lived with a neurological disease that created balance issues. The men almost immediately shifted their attention to Sarah, who appeared not to have a disability, and virtually ignored Jane. This example illustrates how little we understand about people with abilities different from our own. Jane and Sarah did eventually explain their experiment, disclosing that it was, in fact, Sarah who used the crutches, not Jane. A fascinating and enlightening discussion ensued.

Sarah explained, "What's lost on society at large is one critical thing: all of us are 'dis-abled.' It's merely a matter of degree, and how visible that disability is, and how those who are not

visibly disabled respond to it. Although we try to remove struc-
tural barriers, many others still exist. It's good to have a wheel-
chair-user parking space, but what's the point if the building's
interior is not accessible? Common problems include restaurants without wheelchair seating—a common problem in fast
food establishments—or a public bathroom without a properly accessible wheelchair stall. I laugh when I visit bathrooms
that fail the wheelchair-friendly designation: sure, they have
the toilet with a grab bar, but toilet paper is out of reach. The
cut-away sink gets a pass. Still, the soap dispenser and the hand
dryer are out of reach, or the mirror needs repositioning for a
seated person."

Learning how to appropriately relate to people living with
a disability or other challenges is a matter of practice. Taking
the time to understand this raises our awareness of a variety of
difficulties many of us face. Showing compassion to those who
have such challenges is necessary, polite, and civil. Having
self-compassion when faced with any new challenges can be
even more difficult because we judge ourselves too harshly. In
many personal interactions, worrying about how we are doing
doesn't help. Usually we are doing better than we think. Fun-
damentally, we should respect everyone's strengths and weaknesses. It is up to us to treat one another as equals deserving of
dignity and kindness.

So, nod when you pass someone on the sidewalk. Such
kindness accompanied by a smile can make someone's day!

# Pet Peeves

*I don't have pet peeves like some people.*
*I have whole kennels of irritation.*

— Whoopi Goldberg

L et's face it. We all have pet peeves—things that other
people do that irritate us. One of my biggest is men wearing hats (especially baseball caps) indoors. I was never a fan of
ball caps; however, it sends me around the bend when they're
worn inside. A man should automatically remove his hat when
indoors. This gesture shows respect. To not do so is a sign of
disrespect, whether intentional or not.

The problem is that many people simply do not understand
the importance of being respectful. The way to deal with pet
peeves compassionately is to reduce their sting by realizing
that the offender is probably not intentionally annoying you.
Pet peeves push our buttons because they often remind us of
aspects of our own behavior that offend others. Try following The Golden Rule by accepting other people's flaws as we
would want them to accept ours. That reduces our stress and
allows us to move through the moment with grace.

Another of my pet peeves is when someone licks their knife
at the table. Licking a knife is dangerous and makes some peo-

ple feel uncomfortable, whether at the dining table or not. This example tempts us to step in "for safety's sake," but that is not our responsibility. Ignoring the ill manners of others is often the best path to follow. Do not confuse ignoring with accepting or approving. And be sure they don't, either.

Spitting, tossing cigarette butts, or discarding chewing gum on the sidewalk or street are also pet peeves. This behavior shows a total disrespect for public spaces but appears de rigueur these days. As a result, in some places, actual signs admonish such conduct, and in some situations, it can carry a fine. It is the same as littering or leaving one's garbage by the side of the road. As stewards of our communities, we should be mindful of maintaining places so that they're as clean or cleaner for the next person as they were for us. Setting a good example is the best way to achieve this end.

While driving, one of my pet peeves is the reckless maniac who frighteningly cuts in and out of traffic, particularly during rush hour, while completely ignoring the merging protocol. They somehow feel entitled to keep butting in front of other vehicles, as though this bullying behavior will get them to their destination any faster. It is dangerous and rude and shows disrespect for other drivers. It's comparable to honking your horn, that annoying form of communication designed to alert one to danger, not to be a nonverbal chastisement. Then there's the driver who juts out into a street just far enough to make it almost impossible for oncoming traffic to continue. This aggressiveness is dangerous. Courteous and competent driving makes for safer roads.

Another pet peeve concerns men not wearing jackets with neckties and dress shirts at memorial or ceremonial events, especially in church. Although many buildings and halls heat up when crowded, this is not an excuse to take off jackets and ties except under the most extreme circumstances. Today many men are not accustomed to wearing a coat, let alone a necktie, so this extra layer of clothing seems optional. However, they are not optional at certain times, and going to church is one of them.

It's interesting how one person's pet peeve is another's normal behavior. Having pet peeves is a way of seeing faults in others. Perhaps we can feel better about ourselves and avoid doing things that are truly annoying to someone else. Being human, we all have frailties, and we must accept that as truth. Being aware of how we influence those around us can be a big step toward understanding that. Leading by example, which we consciously and unconsciously do, allows us to teach our children, students, and others what we accept as appropriate. This amalgamation of actions is a true reflection of how we live. It's never too late to do our part to make our communities healthy and vibrant by showing respect, civility, and compassion.

# The Art of the Dinner Party: Guests, Eats, and How It All Comes Together

*A party without cake is just a meeting.*

— Julia Child

⁓

D inner parties are marvelous opportunities to bring friends and family together to have fun, meet new people, and introduce your latest culinary conquests. Planning any dinner party involves many steps, beginning with building the guest list. I have hosted or been the guest at many dinner parties over the years and realize just how important it is to put together a good guest list.

For some occasions, the menu determines the guest list, with the food being the primary focus. Let's face it: some people just don't like or cannot eat certain foods. If you're having a special lobster dinner, for example, failing to check before inviting people who may have aversions or allergies to shellfish would seem a bit absent-minded and potentially dangerous.

There are dinner parties where the hosts have spent days cooking an extraordinary meal revolving around a single key ingredient. Lamb cooked five ways is one example. Lobster boils is another. As these events are gastronomic extravaganzas, great attention is paid to the guest list, ensuring everyone would enjoy the fruits of their labors.

Then there are dinner parties where camaraderie is the main focus. In these instances, it is not unusual to have two or three entrees from which to choose. Planning the invitation list for such a get-together involves a different thought process. It is essential to include people who are likely to be congenial, keeping in mind that differing viewpoints add to the life of the party. The larger the party, the more potential for a diverse guest list.

One surefire way to create tension at a dinner party is to have competing strong personalities seated at the same table. My advice is to avoid this at all costs unless your goal is to create such stress. Dueling conversations inevitably result within even the most jaded groups. When dinners include multiple alpha-type personalities, take special care with the seating.

These dinners can be for social or business purposes with agendas ranging from forming a relationship to concluding a critical deal. Either way, arrange the seating to achieve the desired result.

Multiple tables skillfully seated solve this challenge, help orchestrate engaging conversations, and maximize the fun. I enjoy nothing more than bringing together people who have never met. Including people from entirely different backgrounds helps create exciting conversations, an element that enhances any great party.

Family dinnertime can be an opportunity for stimulating conversation, too. I find it helpful to limit topics to cheerful, noncontroversial subjects. Suitable topics include sharing what you did during the day, the exciting insights you realized, and what you are looking forward to experiencing. Resist speaking about things you dislike or that have irritated you during the day, or others' personal traits you find irritating. Save these conversations for more appropriate times away from the dinner table.

Dinnertime is an important chance for the family to get together. We digest food most efficiently in a stress-free environment, so pleasant conversations are in order. Tired, cranky people should resist complaining about their miserable day at work, unappreciative boss, or horrible rush hour traffic. As compassionate as the family may be, it puts a real damper on a relaxing dinner. Discuss anything emotionally charged away from the table.

Enjoying a deliciously prepared meal is one of life's most pleasant activities, as well it should be. After all, if you are going to do something three times a day, you should do it right, eh?

Whether you find yourself hosting a dinner party or being entertained as a guest, this is not always a political arena or a forum for advancing one's philosophies. However, listening to others' opinions and points of view widens our perspectives. We enjoy an atmosphere of true friendship, where respect for one another is the main course. Compassion is the magic ingredient that allows this to happen because it ignites our natural curiosity to understand the world around us with greater clarity. Sharing experiences with others in this way elevates both our trust and our happiness.

# Surprise!

*Those who are easily shocked should be
shocked more often.*

— Mae West

W ho doesn't love a surprise? Wonderful surprises may be just what the doctor ordered: winning the lottery, being stunned by intense beauty, or receiving joyous news! More mundane yet still pleasant surprises are generally well tolerated. Nasty surprises aren't. In either case, they throw us off balance, and our reaction to the sudden change determines its effect on us. Surprises can be compassionate acts when they help relieve suffering. Listening to your inner voice can help you determine if a surprise will produce the desired result.

Practical jokes appear differently from one person to another. The prankster may intend to have some good fun and inject some humor into a situation. However, the recipient may see it differently, and the attempt at humor may turn into a painful moment. Even when no harm is intended, unintentional suffering can result. It can also backfire when the jokester becomes the recipient of a prank in the form of a payback. Here the intent to get even involves putting the other person in their place, which is not funny and is, in fact, disrespectful and rude, especially if done in public. Let's face it: many people do not find surprises or practical jokes amusing.

It is helpful to remember that people may feel embarrassed, hurt, or belittled regardless of whether that is our intention if others witness it. Therefore, if you're planning a practical joke or nasty surprise, do so privately. Thinking through how the whole process will unfold and how it will affect everyone involved will go a long way toward diminishing embarrassment and preventing damage to a relationship.

No one is immune to having their feelings hurt. Eleanor Roosevelt reminds us, "No one can make you feel inferior without your consent." This statement puts the responsibility for and regulation of our emotions clearly in our lap, which is sometimes easier said than done. Err on the side of caution. Put yourself in the other person's shoes before taking action. Having compassion for one another is the surest way to be comforting, caring, and kind. That's what civility is all about.

# Blended Families and Holidays

*You have to take things slowly. Just because you love*
*someone doesn't mean that you're going to love their*
*children automatically. All relationships take time to grow*
*and develop. Be willing to give everyone the time and*
*space that they need. It will come.*

— Kelly LeFurgey

⌁

F amily structures can be complicated and confusing today, particularly as multiple marriages create blended families. Tensions can arise, especially around holidays, weddings, graduation ceremonies, and other celebrations. These command performance events should bring out our best behavior, which can sometimes mean biting your tongue and showing compassion.

Difficult as it may be, we must put our core differences aside in deference to why we have gathered together in the first place. This can be much more challenging for some people than others. If you cannot control your emotions or maintain a level of acceptable civility, then it is best not to accept the invitation in the first place.

Dinner parties involving assorted family members and friends can present challenges to the host when planning a seating chart. Placing potential combatants well apart and out of range of even potential eye contact makes the meal more pleasant for everyone. The host must know the dynamics of the guest list well in advance of the guests' arrival. We usually know where danger may lurk, but we would do well to get the current state of affairs from someone in the know. However, surprises will occur, and it's best to start by defusing any negative vibes as quickly as possible. Remembering to keep our composure in the face of turmoil is the sign of a great host.

Being a great guest can present challenges as well. As somewhat of an extrovert, I like to converse with everyone at most gatherings, including people who may be difficult. Take the high, less traveled road and approach everyone with the same sense of humility and respect.

At weddings, family tensions can arise. Adhering to proper protocol is helpful. First, the host must draw up a guest list in order of importance. In most cases, the relationship between the marrying couple and their guests determines the priority. However, flexibility is necessary, because each family is unique. Remember that weddings are for brides and grooms and for celebration!

Funerals are often highly emotional celebrations of life. Most people attending share great sadness and grief. Funeral arrangements are often the shared responsibility of the deceased's next of kin, the funeral director, and a clergy member. Too often, well-meaning friends and family are actually in the way. Allowing the grieving process to unfold for people in their own way is the compassionate way to handle these stressful times. No two people experience grief or loss in the same way. Kindness goes a long way in letting others understand your true intentions and feelings.

Graduation ceremonies can be stressful events for a variety of reasons. Sometimes, seating is limited. Perhaps the scheduling makes attending difficult. Nonetheless, it's a significant milestone in anyone's life, and we should accord it the proper respect. Emotions can play a role in any celebration like this, and allowing each of us to show our feelings is a compassionate act we can all embrace.

No matter the occasion, we must always keep the real purpose of the gathering in focus. If we do, we will likely think less about ourselves and more about others—it's a foundational principle of civility.

# When Man's Best Friend Moves On

*The reality is that you will grieve forever. You will not "get over" the loss of a loved one; you will learn to live with it. You will heal, and you will rebuild yourself around the pain you have suffered. You will be whole again, but you will never be the same. Nor should you be the same, nor would you want to.*

— Elisabeth Kübler-Ross

F ew things in life are as heart-wrenching as losing a pet. The relationship we enjoy with our pets, no matter how long or short, grabs us in a distinctly different way than the relationships we have with people. Our friends instinctively know how emotionally attached we become to our pets. Still, the depth of this attachment is uniquely personal.

Word spreads very quickly after someone's beloved pet dies. We are saddened as we remember a time when we suffered such a loss ourselves. The sadness and pain can be devastating. During these times of suffering, we most appreciate empathy and compassion from our friends and family.

Respecting the wishes of people who prefer to be left alone during times of grieving is appropriate. We show compassion by allowing them to handle their sorrow privately. Letting people know that we are thinking about them and sending them prayers and good wishes can be enormously helpful.

If you want to acknowledge the loss of someone's pet, sending a card is a nice gesture. Some people prefer to plant a tree or flowering shrub in the pet's memory.

One of my friends places a small bronze plaque in her courtyard's brickwork to memorialize each of her pets. Some of us choose to bury our beloved pets in a pet cemetery. Alternatively, we may want to spread their ashes in a favorite field where they once romped or into a mountain lake where they once enjoyed going for a swim. Some loving owners bury their pets right in their backyard, and others keep their pets' ashes in unique urns on a mantel.

As pet owners, we enjoy many blessings, not the least of which is deciding when their quality of life has slipped to an unacceptable point. We have an innate bond with our pets that allows us to know when that time has come. Having a good relationship with a veterinarian is helpful: a compassionate vet and support staff can make a huge difference.

Each pet is unique. We form an intimate relationship with each one, no matter how many we may have. Pets give us unconditional love throughout their lives, even when we might be undeserving. Honoring their memory is often a helpful way to achieve closure. Over the years, some of us will be lucky enough to have many pets, creating many unique relationships. I believe they await our arrival in the great beyond. It gives us great peace of mind to know they lived happy lives and that their memories live through the trees, bushes, or monuments bearing their names. If all of God's creatures were so lucky, the world would be a kinder, gentler place.

# If Cabinets Could Speak

*It is a narrow mind which cannot look at a subject
from various points of view.*

— George Eliot, *Middlemarch*

M y mother pointed to a photograph of a cabinet she liked
in a book on antiques and said, "That's the one!" She
spoke with a cabinetmaker and asked him to make her an exact
copy of the breakfront she admired. In due course, the cabinet
arrived and took the place of honor in our front hall. Mother
tastefully arranged various treasures behind its glass-paneled
doors. This piece of furniture was illuminated with tiny lights
and looked warm and welcoming.

Although this cabinet cannot reveal all of what it witnessed
over the years, it is symbolic of the pieces of furniture we all
have owned. These pieces, standing sentinel in quiet, statu-
esque solitude, have greeted many people.

My mother's cabinet saw the smiles on my sister's and my
face as we raced down the stairs each Christmas morning. It
saw the terror in my eyes on the days my report card arrived in
the mail. It heard the wrath that ensued from a mother whose
underachieving son was a huge disappointment. It witnessed
the dogs and the guests smelling the orchids, felt the teeth of

a young puppy gnawing at its delicate legs, and heard joyful laughter and sometimes unpleasant remarks.

This cabinet moved many times after my parents divorced as my mother took it from house to house. Eventually, the cabinet became mine to fill with my things. As I have moved through my life, this cabinet has borne witness to another generation of joys, sorrows, new surroundings, and magical moments. I hope it has been happy in my custody.

Those tiny lights burned out, and their replacements burned out over the years. The cabinet's interior became dark as the bulbs went out one by one. Finding new bulbs seemed impossible. I had almost given up.

Then one day, as luck would have it, I was driving the Red Baron (my father's old car) through Worcester, Massachusetts, and the oil light came on. Since this had happened before, I knew it meant I had to pull over immediately and find some oil. I wandered around a bit before finding a service station. Then the trick was finding my way back to the highway. Wouldn't you know that in my wanderings through town I passed a store called Bulbs.com? A proverbial light bulb went off, and I thought they could help me in my quest for tiny lights for the cabinet. After a few minutes of sifting through catalogs online, they located two such bulbs. Of course, they were not in stock and were on back order from Germany. One day, they finally arrived. Rarely have I ever been so excited by a small, padded envelope.

The cabinet took on a whole new life. It seemed to thank me for resurrecting its ability to see so many things it had been unable to see for so long. I arranged a whole new group of objects on the newly illuminated shelves. This time, it was a collection of beautiful tea bowls that sparkled like jewels. They overlooked the newly decorated Windsor House Bar Room.

The cabinet now watches over my friends and me as we ruminate about the world's problems, just as my mother and her friends did. The conversations that have evolved over glasses of Oh Be Joyful or a cup of tea remain hidden in this stronghold of time immemorial. It gives me a great sense of gratitude and comfort every time I turn on the cabinet's tiny lights.

If we look around our houses and our busy lives, we all have silent memory banks that hold many priceless treasures. But their greatest value is sentimental. When we walk by these silent witnesses to our lives, we can reminisce about the times we have shared.

I enjoy taking the time to sit quietly, sometimes alone, and recall bygone days. It brings gratitude back into focus and helps me remember how lucky I am to connect with so many people. These connections are what make us fully human.

Take the time to talk to your cabinets occasionally. They listen, and often they even respond in genuinely comforting ways.

# Civility, Compassion, Culture, and Politics

*In the end, both civility and compassion are a culture issue,
and a focus on building a positive, thriving work environment
is required to instill these qualities in your workforce. Culture
change is a long road, but you can help your organization
create a positive work environment where civility and
compassion are present in everyday interactions, all the time.*

— Catherine Mattice Zundel

There's nothing like an election to stir up emotions. Candidates should want to look their best and focus on the contribution they would make if elected. Instead, they spend a disproportionate amount of effort bashing their opponents to make themselves look better.

This bad behavior can hurt the whole election process and society as a whole. Does it have to be this way? Why does this happen? Can we change the way we engage in the election process to effect positive change? Compassion for their constituents would shift politicians' focus from what is best for their personal agenda to what is best for the public good.

New challenges continually command our attention. The fact that change is constant is something we all experience but often resist as steadfastly as possible. Nonetheless, the status quo will change. New generations of minds will see life and what matters most from perspectives different from their predecessors'. It takes enormous energy to effect a healthy change. Being human is challenging. We are all different; our imperfections make us unique, yet we have many more things in common than we may realize. However, we are living in a society that demands both vigilance and fear. To survive, we created codependent and interdependent societies in which we distinguish one another as either friend or foe. Over the years and for a variety of reasons, human beings have craved and fought for power, originally for survival and procreation. However, over the millennia, the desire for power has become unhealthy, and struggles over it have resulted in the culture of fear in which we now live.

Breaking the cycle that perpetuates this culture of fear requires compassion above all else. This fundamental principle of civility acknowledges our differences as individuals with respect and humility and without judgment. Compassion goes further because it includes the suffering that we all endure. We need to recognize the feelings of loneliness and fear in others as opportunities to show compassion, which can come in many forms of kindness.

Most importantly, compassion is the opposite of oppression and abandonment, two of our most often used defaults. Some people view others' challenges as weaknesses and try to overpower them to mask their own lack of self-worth. Others look the other way, becoming bystanders and putting their proverbial heads in the sand and hoping other people's problems will simply go away. However, more and more people are resonating with the current of compassion slowly but surely embracing society.

In the election process, compassionate candidates stand out because they focus on their strengths and the good things they can do to improve their potential constituents' lives. They do not mock their opponents' missteps. Compassionate leadership can change the culture of fear into a culture of safety in which we can all fulfill our life's passion.

As members of an electorate, we have a right to know where our elected officials stand on matters vital to us. Public forums where people can speak directly to candidates are far more successful than the social media battles that resemble street fights more than civil discourse. Politicians who engage in these mudslinging contests give politics a bad name. More importantly, they reveal themselves as too immature to hold public office.

People rant on social media with thoughtless and incorrect comments. Their remarks fan the flames of divisiveness that pit members of tightly knit communities against each other. This form of emotional cannibalism has got to stop. We can make it stop right now by disengaging from unhealthy discussions and refocusing our attention on important matters and how we can become part of the solution.

As you turn your attention to the next election, observe how candidates comport themselves on social media and in public. Focus on the strengths the candidates can offer your community and the challenges that matter the most to you. The candidate who is the scrappiest and can win the street fight is not as crucial as the candidate who has the most compassion for their constituents. You'll want to decide which candidate will go to bat for you when the chips are down.

# Self-Reflective Exercises

- Are you judgmental? About what?
- Can you forgive yourself and others easily? If not, where are the blocks?
- Can you experience unconditional love?
- Are you too hard on yourself every time you make a mistake?
- Have you been able to exhale today?
- Are you tougher on others than you are on yourself? Is the reverse truer?

*Pillar 3*

# HUMILITY

# Introduction

*True humility is staying teachable*
*regardless of how much you already know.*

— Dana Arcuri

⤳

Many years ago, a group of friends formed an organization similar to the Make a Wish Foundation. Nothing can be more humbling than helping to relieve the suffering of a child who may not reach adulthood. It is a genuine act of kindness to make a wish come true and shower some happiness and provide some temporary relief from life's complex challenges.

However, reading all the applications and deciding from a needs-based assessment whose wishes will come true is a real challenge. The volunteers took up their work with humility and positive intentions to grant wishes, intending to think beyond themselves and consider what their decisions would mean to someone in need of some joy.

We all need to be reminded from time to time that the kindness of others sustains the world. Humility and empathy remind us that on almost every level, we are all equals. The continued success of this group and others testifies to how vital this service is.

Connecting on a level of humility exposes us to ourselves and others in ways that can take us outside our comfort zones.

We gain new perspectives when we allow ourselves to relate with others. We instinctually try to protect ourselves from danger. Still, we learn that we must take chances every once in a while to help others. These connections are often the strongest, most meaningful, and intimate that we ever make.

It is not uncommon in the workplace to hear people bandy around the often-misunderstood word "humility." For this discussion about civility, humility, in essence, is the simple idea that there are no "big shots." No matter our professional position or achievements, or our social station, wealth, or education, we are all of great value. This is not to say that we cannot hold certain people in higher regard than others or that we might feel like our lives are less fulfilling than others. But remember that when the shoe is on the other foot and we help others lead more satisfying lives, we are held in high regard more than we may ever know.

In some businesses, healthy teamwork is vitally important. Yet this dynamic is unhealthy in too many workplaces today. A weak sense of purpose and personal fulfillment can severely affect a company's bottom line. A lack of humility, especially at the highest levels, causes many of the best employees to leave in search of organizations where they would hopefully feel valued.

An emotionally intelligent company would have no appetite for this frightening attrition and would act quickly to reverse it. Sadly, changing such a dynamic within a toxic company takes time. Sometimes it never happens. In the meantime, scores of employees' lives are negatively affected. Is this how we want to be treating one another? Think about it!

Take a moment to consider humility in the context of where you work, especially if you are the boss. We measure good leaders by their ability to make their employees feel valued. If there is a weak link in your business, taking a look at your humility meter might be a good idea.

Humility is a human quality that is evident at home, on the ball field, and at work. Learning humility and kindness should begin at home. Those not raised to believe that all of us are equal need to stop and, as any GPS will instruct, recalculate! Don't we wish for the next generation to live in a compassionate world with a sustainable social order where everyone practices humility?

# Common Courtesy

*I appreciate people who are civil, whether they mean it or not. I think: Be civil. Do not cherish your opinion over my feelings. There's a vanity to candor that isn't really worth it. Be kind.*

— Richard Greenberg

Do you ever feel like you don't have the time or energy to be available to others as much as you would like to be? It happens to almost all of us. Time flies by so fast sometimes that it seems like there isn't time enough to accomplish what we have set out to do each day. We often just run out of time. Is it poor time management, good old-fashioned stress, or a sense of being overwhelmed?

Acts of kindness to reduce this stress make us feel good about ourselves, are amazingly helpful to others, and are basic elements of common courtesy. These kindnesses prevailed in the good old days when life moved at a slower pace without all the electronic aids of the 21st century, a time when downtime meant quality time with friends and family. We seemed to have more energy then. With a little planning, we can return to a slower pace.

When someone shows us common courtesy or politeness, we generally feel happier. Someone who helps a senior citizen struggling with their grocery bags makes a good impression. Many people might just walk right by. Other gestures can be as simple as making an effort to look someone in the eye, smiling at the solitary person sitting on the park bench, or greeting others cordially upon entering a room. These people display kindness and grace, and I am always thankful for my contact with them. These common courtesies are the small gestures that enrich our lives.

Writings about random acts of kindness abound. These usually short articles always give a warm, fuzzy feeling because of how we relate to these thoughtful gestures. One time, I went through a tollbooth and gave two fares to the attendant: one for me and the other for the car behind me. That time I knew the other driver. It was a fun and unexpected perk to brighten up her day. She later thanked me and mentioned that she had continued paying it forward with the car behind her! I have done that since then, without knowing who the driver behind me was. I never receive thanks, save for perhaps the flashing of headlights, but the thrill is the same.

How would this act of kindness influence our lives if we did this every day? What if doing random acts of kindness became a lifestyle? How many arguments could we avoid? How much good energy could we generate? If we reflected on this for a moment and decided to try it, I guarantee we would feel quite different about our everyday interactions with everyone in our lives. Helping in simple, generous ways positively affects us all.

Critical components of these kinds of considerations are awareness and common sense. Looking beyond our world, we should notice when someone might benefit from a helping hand, a leg up, a genuine smile, or a nod of acknowledgment. As a courteous person, you observe people as you enter a room. You automatically do this when a waiter approaches your table to take your order or when you approach a traffic intersection.

Awareness naturally leads to action. It is usually pretty clear what needs our attention. Take a moment to open the door for a mother carrying her baby. Move your car a little bit so someone else can park, too. Acknowledge your sister's shy boyfriend with a smile and some conversation. Apologize if you bump into someone; better yet, be aware that someone is nearby and avert a collision.

A third essential component of consideration is giving of yourself and not expecting anything in return. Thanks comes from doing and knowing that you have been a kind person. People may not even notice, much less return the kindness, but you can take heart knowing that you are creating the kind of world you want to live in by your actions.

As you go through your hectic day, remember to be aware of others, lend a hand when needed, and help wanting nothing in return. Through these small actions, you make the world a better place for everyone.

# Agree to Disagree

*A pessimist sees the difficulty in every opportunity; an optimist sees the opportunity in every difficulty.*

— Winston Churchill

As a professional etiquette expert, I engage in in-person and online discussions about good manners and protocol not only with clients, but also with colleagues. Some of the more revealing conversations involve different traditions, with subjects varying between topics such as conducting a business meeting or dining with friends and family. Opinions on various guidelines can vary even among so-called experts. This conflict can lead to confusion when simple questions arise, such as when to help someone with their chair; what to do with your napkin when leaving the table; or where to lay dessert cutlery in a table setting. These discussions can turn into a real tug-of-war and remain unresolved.

This same pattern of behavior occurs in many aspects of our lives. Sometimes differing points of view are subtle and of little consequence. In the minds of those holding them, though, they become larger than life and worth defending to the end. But how many of these critically important matters do we even remember a week later? It is worth reminding ourselves of this point when we begin to feel our blood pressure rise as we prepare our defenses.

One feeling we all embrace is acceptance. To maintain healthy, sustainable communities, we need to trust one another. We rely on other people for many reasons. There are modern-day hunters and gatherers, warriors and guardians, teachers and sages. They are the folks who grow our crops, and prepare, process, package, and give us our daily bread. They are the protectors of our borders and help preserve our chosen way of life. They allow one generation to follow another with the knowledge and wisdom needed to maintain a healthy society. The more accepting and understanding we are of others the happier life is.

Today, there seems to be a growing need to be correct. As we rush through our busy schedules, we make time to be sure that those around us accept us and agree with us. The idea that our beliefs and principles are the only right ones leads to division. Ironically this belief also leads us on the path to rejection. Who wants that?

To strike a balance that we can all live with, we eventually realize that we may need to compromise on some of our firmly held ideas. This give-and-take doesn't mean that we have to compromise our value systems, but we must learn to listen to other voices as well as develop the ability to agree to disagree.

Herein lies the pathway to compassion, not only for others but also for ourselves. We need to give ourselves a break, to take time out, or simply chill. As we develop this ability, we realize that we have a deep respect for each other. When we understand that a healthy society can be homogeneous if we are respectful of each other, our lives can become more relaxed and we become more accepting of those around us without necessarily agreeing with everything they think, say, or do.

Whether at work or home, we should be more aware of when we behave like this ourselves. By noticing when and why we take specific actions or make absolute statements, we can begin to change them. We can start to set examples for our children and our friends of being more tolerant and compassionate.

One benefit of not always being right is that we don't have the responsibility of upholding and even defending our beliefs. Let the other person be correct for a change. Take time out now and again. It's amazing how, when we put other people ahead of ourselves, our lives change for the better and our self-esteem improves. Agreeing to disagree can make for a kinder, gentler world.

# Hospice and Palliative Care

*If we listen and observe carefully, the dying can teach us*
*important things that we need to learn in preparing for the*
*end of our own life's journey.*

— Robert L. Wise

Caring for our family and friends as they reach the final stages of their lives can be stressful, frightening, and physically, mentally, and emotionally overwhelming. As we enter uncharted territory during these challenging times, we can fall prey to inappropriate coping behavior. We are fortunate that most communities have access to supportive services, including visiting nurses, hospices, and residences. Many skilled and well-trained professionals dedicate their lives to helping others make their journey at the end of their path less frightening and less burdensome. When a close friend experienced the benefits of such support, he said, "They go above and beyond, daily fielding questions from patients, family, and friends about what is happening and what to expect as things progress as the end nears."

The process of actively dying can take several days, depending on the person. Hopefully this includes hospice services, which can help ease the dying process with palliative care to reduce suffering in the patient as well as loved ones. It's beneficial for someone to take the lead as the responsible decision maker. Although that person may not carry the responsibility for day-to-day care, they can decide when to seek hospice support services. When possible, make these decisions in advance, as it makes the transition easier.

Although sibling rivalry is as old as humanity itself, humility dictates that we set aside disagreements and respect the crisis at hand. This truce also comes in handy at weddings, funerals, and graduations. These stressful times can challenge us to keep our emotions in check.

Long distances can also add to the stress of a situation. We tend to feel frustrated and unsettled if we cannot be there to assist. Keeping the patient's wishes in mind is of the utmost importance and should help us focus more on our loved ones than on ourselves.

Caring for someone at home can be a lengthy ordeal. Over time we can begin to take many of the small tasks that caregivers do for granted. Make a point of showing gratitude to these folks every day. They are loving human beings. Sometimes, nurses may be attending two or three actively dying patients at one time, and their emotions can become raw. It helps if family members of the dying, even in their time of need, are mindful of caregivers' trials. A comforting word to them is always an appreciated blessing.

Accepting help when we need it can be very empowering. It provides a healthy perspective, allowing us to be more compassionate and understanding of everyone involved. Giving each other enough space to think and grieve promotes the grace and kindness we would want for ourselves.

Caring for people in need is foreign territory for us, especially when we are younger. But as time moves along, most of us will have the responsibility of looking after our aging loved ones. Luckily there are great support systems in place. We can significantly improve our ability to help if we remain humble and remember to put other people's feelings ahead of our own.

# *Volunteerism*

*In helping others, we shall help ourselves, for whatever good
we give out completes the circle and comes back to us.*

— Flora Edwards

H oliday celebrations can be fertile grounds for cultivating humility, compassion, and respect when we assist less fortunate members of our community. These golden opportunities also teach our children the meaning of sharing by bringing joy to others. Volunteerism offers many ways to help, including providing food, donating warm clothes, and visiting people who live alone. Thinking of this assistance as a "leg up" focuses our intention on the true meaning of giving and sharing.

Volunteerism comes in many forms. By extending ourselves with humility we get a lift spiritually, mentally, and emotionally, creating a better world as we do so. Learning to volunteer when we are young helps us develop a sense of belonging within our community. My first volunteer job was visiting with a blind woman living in a convalescent home. It was one of the most depressing places I had ever been in my life, but I would not have missed that weekly visit for anything. She looked forward to my time with her, and I learned so much, including a bit of Braille.

Since those teenage years, I have held a warm spot in my heart for the elderly and people with particular challenges and disabilities. As I grew older, I was able to help more. I still give of my time and resources and encourage others to share their unique talents with people who could benefit. Volunteering gives us a deep sense of connection and respect for others.

# Coloring Outside the Lines

*Hold your head up. Take an unplanned road trip. Be*
*thankful. Try everything once. Color outside the lines. Fall*
*in love. Embrace change. Trust in yourself. Do what you*
*love—dance when everyone is looking. Eat dessert first. Be*
*nice to everyone and send thank you cards. Be the change*
*you wish to see in the world. Play in the rain. Break the*
*rules once in a while. Do random acts of kindness and*
*forgive even when it's hard. Make time for family. Don't*
*count the minutes, count the laughs.*

— Unknown

One of the most fun activities I enjoyed in kindergarten was coloring. We were handed pages with black outlined shapes on which we could add whatever colors we wanted. I learned to avoid coloring outside the lines. However, there is the notion that coloring outside the lines shows creativity and courage. How we learn about boundaries can be a challenge, but one we all must attempt.

We have boundaries in many situations that are more sophisticated than those in coloring books. We set boundaries for ourselves that we don't want others to cross. For example, how far apart do we stand from one another when shaking hands? Are personal questions acceptable? A whole spectrum of behaviors defines who we are and what we find comfortable.

Being civil, understanding what "off-limits" means, and un-covering fertile ground for building relationships are all part of how we conduct our lives. Understanding our boundaries helps us appreciate others as well.

How many times have we thought, *That's none of my business,* or perhaps, *That's none of your business?* These are clear-cut examples of when we cross boundaries or someone crosses ours.

We consider it rude and insensitive when people step over that invisible line. We should remember that others feel the same way when we cross their boundaries. For example, con-sider gossip, which at times becomes the center of conversa-tion. More often than not, gossip does more than communicate factual information: its intent is to empower the messenger ei-ther by demeaning someone else or sharing private personal information, usually with only half-truths, often with blatant falsehoods. Unfortunately, it's very easy to get swept up in this dynamic. It also tends to make us uncomfortable.

While talking recently with a friend, the question came up about how to react to gossip. Do you call gossipers on their behavior on the spot and embarrass them into changing the subject?

When people say hurtful things, let them know that their remarks made you feel uncomfortable. People rarely want to evoke this type of reaction, so they will likely avoid it in the future. Above all, your comment places the ball in their court. From then on, they will make a conscious choice of whether to offend by gossiping. A rule of thumb when speaking about others is never to speak about anyone who is not present to defend themselves.

Slowing down and not speaking without thinking through how others might feel would go a long way toward maintaining healthy relationships. We can then grow and live happier, more fulfilling lives ourselves. We can become more aware of others' feelings as we learn more about our own. Putting other people ahead of ourselves is a good thing to do sometimes. It is also an excellent behavior to pass along to our children.

It's smart to teach children about boundaries at an early age. It also helps establish positive self-esteem. From this, our authentic selves can emerge, and mutual respect for others becomes a natural consequence.

Respecting boundaries allows us to make friends more easily. We build trust through this respect. As we build trust, we begin to feel more relaxed and comfortable forming relationships. It further demonstrates that we consider ourselves equals. Initially, this can be a very humbling experience, especially if we grew up in a world of entitlement. Discovering one another's boundaries carries some risk. This risk softens when we enter new relationships with humility and respect.

# Being of Service to Our Communities

*Always render more and better service than is expected of*
*you, no matter what your task may be.*

— Og Mandino

Few things in life are as gratifying as helping someone achieve something they wish to accomplish. For example, I know that when I first dropped my training wheels and pedaled down the street on two wheels, my father was beaming. He felt as though he had helped me reach an important milestone. As trivial as learning to ride a bicycle may seem, it is symbolic of achieving a goal. How many people remember when they could first tie their shoes or walk the dog or empty the trash? These small steps are all part of growing up and becoming responsible adults.

Likewise, as we mature and become contributing members of society, we have an innate urge to connect with other people and be accepted. To do this successfully, we must establish trust with one another. This dynamic of trusting each other lasts throughout our lives.

As we make connections with people, we learn who we can trust and who we can't. In healthy communities, trusting one another is a way of life. In toxic or dangerous communities, we live in a state of fear, always looking over our shoulders for the next confrontation. Take a moment to check how you feel about living in your community, attending school, or going to work. Do you feel safe, anxious, or in danger? Are you living and working in a community where you get support when you need it?

As responsible, compassionate human beings, we need to be as engaged as possible in our communities. We have to become aware of those in need of help and step in and offer assistance in whatever way we can. Our abilities to support one another vary. Some of us are suited to helping people with physical problems; others are more effective as listeners and advisers, helping with mental and emotional challenges. Most of us can and do help build healthier communities. We must recognize that each of us plays a part in making a safe, kind, and prosperous environment for everyone.

For example, in New Brunswick, Canada, as in many other parts of North America, we face growing challenges in delivering health care. The horror stories in the headlines point out that there is a severe lack of understanding of what it means to "do the right thing," especially when it comes to physical and psychological safety in the workplace. Nurses have shared stories with me that make it abundantly clear that the health care system is in a state of disrepair. It is incumbent upon us as citizens to speak up and act in ways that change such scenarios.

Several years ago, a number of rural Canadians living in Charlotte County, NB, rose up in peaceful protest against the local hospital's operating room closure. The protest was effective and directly caused government leaders to reconsider the decision. Significant changes can result when the management company recalculates its communications and accountability. Further, by listening, it can become more sensitive to and aware of any dangers to its employees' physical, mental, and emotional health. This way managers can make significant changes in how they approach the overall well-being of their employees and customers.

There are many ways in which we can be of service to our communities. Every day, hundreds of not-for-profit organizations depend on volunteers to survive. There is something for everyone, and everyone should volunteer in their community at some point in their lives. Many of us do this to maintain, support, and enhance where we live. It makes us feel good.

Being of service teaches us all six pillars of civility. We learn to have compassion for others and ourselves. We practice humility and are aware of how we affect others and how they affect us. We become responsible citizens, helping to turn those in need in our communities into pillars of strength; gratitude becomes a driving force. By our example, we encourage others to carry on a strong sense of volunteerism and service to our communities. Volunteering is a vital tool for our sustainability and growth. Finding a niche that engages you fully can help you find and fulfill your passion in the most miraculous ways. "If not now, when?"

# Self-Reflective Exercises

- Do you believe that you are better than other people? Have you more confidence, ability, good looks, etc.?
- Do you believe that you are not as good as many people? Have you a lack of confidence, self-worth, ability, good looks, etc.?
- Do you find yourself judging and comparing yourself with others? Why is that important to you?
- Do people hold you in high regard? How do you know? How does that make you feel?

# Pillar 4

# GRATITUDE

# Introduction

*Let us be grateful to the people who make us happy; they*
*are the charming gardeners who make our souls blossom.*

— Marcel Proust

⌒

Gratitude is a state of mind, a feeling that can blossom into
an action. Such action can be thanking someone for their
kindness or sitting quietly and experiencing a sense of appreciation. But to be fully realized, gratitude is a two-way street.

"Thank you" is one of the first phrases we teach our children. Culturally, showing gratitude is important and plays a
vital role in civil society. If we become numb to gratitude, a
domino effect occurs and civility unravels, and with it an aban-
doning of awareness, compassion, and humility.

Unfortunately, a sense of entitlement can encroach on our
encounters, causing us to abandon our manners and what it
means to take a moment to give thanks. We take too much for
granted, from our health to food and shelter, good friends, and
a comfortable lifestyle. I wonder what the world would be like
if we took some time every day to be grateful for our many
blessings, including life itself.

Many people feel strongly enough about the importance of
expressing gratitude that they offer daily opportunities online
for us to share what we are grateful for in writing. Every day
I receive morning emails reminding me to express my grati-

tude. I often start the New Year off by writing a short phrase or sentence about what I appreciate. It may be something as simple as a good friend, the warmth of sunshine on my face, or a delicious meal. I don't think I'm alone in feeling that I should acknowledge gratitude only for something significant, but that isn't the case. We should be grateful for everything—big and small alike.

Although it is sometimes difficult, if not impossible, to be thankful, the truth is that even life's most difficult challenges deserve it. Without these moments in our lives, we would not grow or develop.

Gratitude is also a critical component in any healthy, sustainable work environment. It must come from the top down, flow freely, and be enthusiastically encouraged. Gratitude is contagious. When sincerely expressed, it has the unique power to transform an uninspired business and workplace into a productive, profitable one. Gratitude serves as a vital nutrient to everything it touches.

In the highly competitive business environment in which most of us work, praise is often in short supply, but the need for it is tremendous. Employees work far more effectively when they know their work is appreciated. Acknowledgment that their work is "a job well done" must be delivered every day. Bosses who do not take the time to praise workers, colleagues, and clients are not using their most powerful tool effectively.

The positive results of gratitude happen every day. It is up to us to take the time to express appreciation and to receive the benefits of being grateful. Stop and notice what is around you and see the goodness in the people you meet each day. You'll come away with a feeling of peace. Perhaps you'll even discover something new to be grateful for.

# Saying Thank You

*As we express our gratitude, we must never forget that the highest appreciation is not to utter words but to live by them. We must find time to stop and thank the people who make a difference in our lives.*

— John F. Kennedy

⌐ ๑ ⌐

We have become too casual when it comes to expressing thanks. It seems as though it's just too much trouble sometimes. The thought that a missed thank-you note will go unnoticed is an unwise assumption. A senior partner in a law firm once mentioned to me how much he appreciated the thank-you note he had received from a junior associate he and his wife had entertained at their home. More notable, however, was that the thank-you note was the only one they received. This gesture demonstrates just how appreciated a thoughtful, handwritten thank-you note can be. The guest did not take the hospitality he had received for granted.

We race through life without "smelling the roses." Considering the amount of time and effort others spend on entertaining us and showing us a good time, perhaps by preparing a favorite meal or hosting a party at a favorite restaurant, it only makes sense to receive this hospitality with grace and respect. Slow down when you have the chance. You will enjoy life's experiences, and saying thank you will roll off your tongue or out of your pen easily.

Getting off on the right foot makes writing these notes a snap. Here's how it's done.

- Buy a box or two of good-quality note cards at a stationery store. Get heavy, plain stock with lined envelopes. Use them for writing special notes to friends. Always keep a box on hand.
- Purchase a good-quality ink pen and use it when writing personal notes.
- Keep the notes short and to the point. Remember, this is a note thanking someone for something they have given you or done for you. It's not about you as much as it is about them. People like being appreciated. It strengthens friendships and shows respect.
- Write your thank-you notes promptly, within 48 hours of opening a gift or experiencing whatever it is you are thankful for. As children, my sister and I would sit down together and write our notes the day after Christmas. Because it was a tradition, we simply did it alongside our mother.
- If you make mistakes on the note, start over. Soon you learn to slow down when writing, and errors become rare. After all, these are notes, not manuscripts; a few short sentences will suffice.
- Be sincere about your message. Showing gratitude in our time-hungry lives has taken a back seat as a priority. We have learned to take for granted the many kindnesses others show us. It's time to reorder that list.

- Don't throw away gift tags. It's easy to forget which gift came from which aunt or uncle. If you hope to remain on the receiving end of their generosity, thank them for the specific present they gave you.
- Poor handwriting is not an excuse for not writing a note. Even though many people don't learn proper penmanship in schools today, most of us can print legibly. And practice makes perfect. Writing more slowly makes for a much neater look.
- Handwrite the envelopes, including your return address. Computer-generated labels are impersonal and the lazy way out. Just think of how lovely it is to receive a fully hand-addressed envelope in the mail. You, too, can provide this experience to others!
- If you have children, teach them how to write thank-you notes. Be gentle with your direction. Engage them by having them choose their own stationery at the store or online. Make this fun by including a trip to the post office, where children can select commemorative stamps for their cards!

I have been writing thank-you notes since I was about eight years old. Strange as it may seem, I wish I were better at it. Reaching out to connect with people with gratitude should not be awkward. It takes some practice, but it's well worth the effort.

# An Ideal Traveler

*Travel is fatal to prejudice, bigotry,*
*and narrow-mindedness.*

— Mark Twain

There is nothing I enjoy more than traveling. I love exploring new places, revisiting favorite haunts, and enjoying
the company of old friends wherever they may be. Having
owned and operated an inn and restaurant for several years, I
have seen the hospitality business from both the proprietor's
and the guest's viewpoint.

One of the keys to a successful vacation or even a short visit
is to have a plan. Many travelers like to "wing it" on the road,
and I am all in favor of that. For some people, it adds to the sus-
pense and adventure. For others, it allows flexibility that a se-
ries of reservations would preclude. But a plan, however loose,
does help avoid disappointment and nasty surprises. Knowing
where you want to end up for the evening gives you a goal.

It is advisable to call for reservations a few days in advance.
If you have a room booked, remember that there is often no one
on duty around the clock, especially at small inns or bed-and-
breakfast establishments. If you are going to be late, call ahead
and let someone know. If you must cancel at the last minute,

expect to pay for your booking anyway. Remember that a no-show is real money out of the innkeeper's pocket.

Well-run establishments will often ask you what time you plan to arrive and explain how late someone will be available to check you in. This information helps innkeepers have the appropriate staff on hand to settle you into your room. They will also likely ask if you are traveling with pets or small children. Be up front with them. Surprising hosts with extra people in your party is unfair, disrespectful, and likely to lead to disappointment. The adage "the guest is always right" does not apply here. Do not assume that there are smoking facilities, that pets are welcome (even the most perfectly behaved ones that do not shed or bark), or that cots or pull-out sofas are available.

Even though guests are paying customers, they are not entitled to unreasonable requests. If you have special needs or requirements, by all means discuss them with the manager or host in advance. Most are willing to accommodate guest requirements if it's at all possible. That is, after all, what the hospitality business is all about.

One of the benefits of staying in smaller establishments is that the innkeepers are likely to be familiar with local attractions and local restaurants. This knowledge makes it possible for them to make recommendations to fit your taste and pocketbook. Larger hotels can rely on temporary staff, who may be less familiar with local attractions, especially in resort towns. Local businesses often place brochures and other information about their establishments with local accommodations. Using this information will help you get the most out of your visit.

If you have clear ideas about what you want to see or be near, inquire ahead of time when deciding where to stay in a particular town or region. For example, if you might require a pharmacy or access to a medical facility, see to it that you will not be in for a surprise. If you are traveling with small children or pets, make sure that whatever services you might anticipate needing, such as a babysitter or veterinarian, are available. Likewise, if you want to be in a pet-free, adults-only place, ask when making your plans. Careful planning can make a real difference.

Good service is also, to some degree, a function of gratitude. If you are staying somewhere and you like your host, your room, your meal, or the service in general, be sure to leave a positive comment about your experience. Innkeepers and their staff appreciate it when guests show their gratitude with a thank-you or even a kind social media review. I advise leaving a cash tip in your bedroom for the housekeeper. If an accident occurs in your room, such as a broken lamp or a stained carpet, let the host know before you leave so that they can quickly address the problem. If you approach travel as a two-way street where both the innkeeper and you as the guest are in this activity together, your time away from home will be more enjoyable.

# Collaboration

*It takes two flints to make a fire.*

— Louisa May Alcott, *Little Women*

Nothing is as essential to human beings as the need to connect with one another. As a species, we depend on connecting for our very survival, as most species do. Healthy connections are what make our lives fulfilling, successful, and enjoyable.

For most of us, our work life occupies about a third of our time, maybe more. If we take on an entrepreneur's mantle, the opportunities to connect with other like-minded folks abound. As a result, we discover that we can increase our efficiency, abilities, and profitability through collaboration.

New Brunswick, where I live, is a fertile ground for many small businesses that have discovered the numerous benefits of collaborating on reaching a common goal. One of my roles is to advise on the etiquette needed to make such collaborations successful.

One of the most important factors is the collective desire for all stakeholders to succeed in ways that would be impossible to achieve as individuals. This belief means taking the position that you want your partners to succeed as much as you.

This decision is one way to help ensure the project gets off the ground and soars.

Another factor is awareness. In this fast-paced world, we can become easily distracted, even derailed from our focus. Our business seemingly runs itself. Since this is impossible, the more time we spend making conscious choices and being aware of the people and events taking place around us, the better positioned we are to succeed. Raising our awareness of the effect we have on everyone with whom we interact and the effect they have on us helps us understand and incorporate the next piece of the puzzle, which is gratitude.

We need to be grateful. The world of business is overflowing with people who seem to view the world from a position of entitlement. This attitude hobbles the ability to be thankful. We express gratitude when we feel understood and appreciated, as we are contributors to the process. Without gratitude, we take everything for granted, we show little respect for our colleagues, and we become isolated, things that are counterproductive to collaboration.

We must clearly understand that we are entitled to precious little and do not merely deserve things. Deepak Chopra once said, "If one feels like one deserves something, one cannot have gratitude for it."

Another factor that is essential to a successful collaboration is compassion. People remain confused about turning compassion into action. Understanding that compassion is more about other people than about us makes implementing this action much more likely.

Many of us think of compassion only as pity or empathy. However, this perspective is only a piece of the whole meaning. It is essential to maintain compassion for ourselves as well as those around us. We are human beings, and in the world of business we can be overly aggressive. The reward becomes the sole focus of our journey rather than the journey itself. We set impossible targets for ourselves and find that we instinctively lay blame on other people or outside circumstances when we fall short of our goals. That is not the sign of a true leader or a good team player.

Finally, we need to take responsibility for what is ours and learn to discern what is not. In other words, mind your own business. As part of any collaborative effort, we should delegate responsibilities with confidence and accountability. Yes, there is usually a point person where the buck stops, but along the way, people must be encouraged to take responsibility for their actions but not feel compelled to control everything else. We all know control freaks, office bullies, and know-it-alls; these folks fail miserably at collaborations.

If you are considering collaborating with someone on a project, you could be in for one of the most rewarding experiences of your life. Few connections are as satisfying in business as working together with others to achieve a common goal. As with most things in life, if we follow the Golden Rule and use a bit of common sense, the sky's the limit!

# How Safe Is Your Workplace?

*Is your workplace psychologically safe? This is the
question that everyone in an organization, at every level,
should be asking in a critical way.*

— Andrew Faas

A fter 25 years in her profession, a practicing nurse told me
of a harrowing experience that caused her to be on medical leave because of a physical injury and resulting post-trau-
matic stress syndrome. A known dangerous patient had severely beaten her, and the rest of the inadequately trained staff had
tried to fend off the patient until help arrived. Sadly, this story
continues across North America. We must find permanent solutions to adequately address the problem of workplace safety.
In the most dangerous and stressful jobs, such as military, law
enforcement, and health care, it is common practice to turn a
blind eye and dismiss traumatic events as part of the job.

The more I learn about how often employers ignore, under-
mine, and consider employees as disposable commodities, the
more I wonder how these leaders sleep at night. The almighty
dollar outweighs the value of humanity and civility. Moving
forward, a company's culture should help determine its worth
as reflected in its employee engagement and retention, as well
as its record on physical, mental, and psychological safety.

To better understand the dynamics involved in handling mental health issues, I read through The Action Plan for Mental Health in New Brunswick 2011–2018. In the letter of introduction it says, "The specific initiatives outlined in this plan will help the government create a system that is responsive to individual and community needs and recognize the importance of continued input of persons experiencing mental illness and their loved ones. These initiatives will be built on the key principles of diversity, dignity, equality, excellence, holism, hope and partnership. They will involve greater collaboration amongst varying departments and jurisdictions of government, educators, employers and non-governmental organizations" (https://www.gnb.ca).

Nowhere is there any mention of employees and the safety issues they face. I was not surprised, because governments and far too many (if not most) other organizations and companies treat their employees like second-class citizens and lesser stakeholders, or as undesirable disposable deadwood.

I have not been able to find anyone with whom this does not resonate and who does not see these inhumane attitudes and practices as unacceptable. Either they've experienced this abusive treatment firsthand or someone they know can clearly describe how fearful and intimidated many employees feel.

This example is not to paint everyone with the same broad brush. Some companies do value their employees as much as their customers or vendors. Employees at such companies love their jobs for this very reason and look forward to working every day.

Don't be fooled by employee satisfaction surveys or other human resources departments' tools to accurately reveal the truth. Often, employees won't participate in such surveys, unless they are conducted by a third party, for fear of losing their jobs if they answer the questions honestly. Human resources departments are often a large part of the problem and are shrouded in cover-ups and deflection. The culture of every organization is rooted in the very top management: the CEOs. These are the people who have the final say, set the tone for the operation, and can make or destroy lives.

When you consider working for or investing in companies, you may want to research how much they value their employees and their success. Companies that place a high value on employee engagement and retention will invariably also produce a greater profit.

Let's engage in the revolution taking place where companies and organizations act in the best interests of all stakeholders to create physically and psychologically safe, supportive, and productive businesses. After all, we spend most of our waking hours working. Employees should not have to live in fear and intimidation! We deserve better and can achieve this together.

# Giving

*Attitude is a choice. Happiness is a choice. Optimism is a choice. Kindness is a choice. Giving is a choice. Respect is a choice. Whatever choice you make makes you. Choose wisely.*

— Roy T. Bennett

During the holidays, many people focus on gift giving. Often we think more about tangible objects than about the gifts of friendship, peace, and gratitude. Sadly, today's commercialism has taken gift giving to a whole new level.

Parents often give gifts to their children during the holidays as substitutes for the love or close emotional connections they miss throughout the year. This cultural deviation has gone unchecked for several generations and, for many, is now the expected norm; it's a sad commentary on today's society.

Traditions for exchanging gifts have also changed. There appears to be more of a focus on what we receive than on what we give. This dynamic leads to all kinds of upheavals of civility. Has gift giving gradually become a responsibility of sorts? Have we lost all sense of humility along the way? Has a sense of entitlement eclipsed our sense of gratitude? Perhaps this is so. I hope that somehow returning to a less materialistic exchange might improve matters.

A gentleman I once spoke with at Christmas dinner told me about a lovely old family tradition. To level the playing field, each member brought identical gifts: Uncle George brought everyone a box of chocolates, or Aunt Sarah got everyone a decorative candle. However, the message with each gift was different and thoughtful, as were the thanks that followed. This exchange served to strengthen personal connections while allowing everyone to focus on individual relationships. This example won't work for everyone, but the point is that the message and feeling behind the gift is more important than the gift itself.

It is critically important to take time out of our busy lives to express our feelings to one another, especially our close friends and family. We tend to take our relationships for granted most of the year, with the occasional birthday or holiday celebration to refocus for a moment. I very much liked the man's story. It reminds me of a tradition in my family known as New Year's Calling, where the men from various family groups call on the women on New Year's Day, giving a box of candy or home-made jam as a symbol of friendship and peace.

In contrast, someone recently asked me to weigh in on parental gift giving. "I buy both my parents Christmas gifts and birthday gifts. What is the etiquette for their gift buying? Should I expect each of them to give me a gift, or at least combine the value into one gift?"

Remember that gift giving is optional. Although exchanging gifts is usual, it is not a rule written in stone. It is your choice to give a gift. Assumptions, expectations, and gifts don't always mix. Give from your heart. Don't worry about receiving anything in return.

What is a gift, after all? It's interesting to note how we feel at other times of the year when we give our friends tokens of friendship springing from the heart. We often get much more of a sense of connection from giving spontaneously than from what has evolved as the obligatory and expected holiday gift.

In the true spirit of Christmas, two of my friends contribute to various charities in honor of each other. They each pick three or more causes they want to support. Their gifts to each other are usually acknowledged with a card from the charity. The friends' attitude is that Christmas is truly a time of giving, particularly to those most in need.

We all love giving and receiving gifts. We cannot overstate or over-practice the meaning behind the spirit of providing peace and gratitude. I hope we all have many opportunities to be generous. If we focus on why we are giving, with no assumptions or expectations about what we may receive in return, our connections will strengthen within our hearts and our families and communities.

# Thanksgiving Deconstructed

*Appreciation is a wonderful thing. It makes what is*
*excellent in others belong to us as well.*

— Voltaire

M ost of us experienced Thanksgiving differently in 2020
because of COVID-19. Some of us may have liked this
break in routine; others didn't. Nonetheless, this pause in tradition, for however long it continues, gave us a chance to reflect
on what Thanksgiving is all about and how we might reconsider celebrating it in years to come.

Thanksgiving has always focused on gratitude. The harvest-
ed crops allow us to enjoy nature's bounty to its fullest. For
this, we prepare a feast and give thanks to a higher power as
recipients of this blessing.

Canada hasn't commercialized this holiday to the extent
the United States has; however, it is a national holiday in both
countries. Many of us remember our less fortunate brothers
and sisters at this time as a gentle reminder of just how blessed
we are. Thanksgiving also shines a light on the responsibility
each of us has to look after each other. When I was growing up,
our family shopped and prepared food hampers filled with everything needed for a full turkey dinner with all the fixings. We

gave a hamper to each employee in appreciation of their many kindnesses throughout the year.

Traditionally, large family gatherings marked this holiday and served as a great reason to bring fledgling branches of the family back together as a sort of annual pilgrimage and re-bonding opportunity. Although 2020 changed all that for many of us, advanced technology allowed many of us to enjoy sitting down at the table together virtually, wherever we were in the world. So even though it is different, reaching out to one another is easily achieved today. In tough times like this, reaching out can make a far bigger difference than we may ever know. Many people are struggling with feeling lonely and isolated.

COVID-19 has only exacerbated the loneliness epidemic that has enfolded society for decades. We know people who find themselves alone for a variety of reasons. Some people may prefer to be by themselves most of the time, but most do not and are either too worried about being an inconvenience or too entrenched in their suffering to understand the negative effects that isolation can have both mentally and physically. These are the folks who can benefit the most during holidays. Their past holds fond memories of family gatherings and feasts when multiple generations would share stories and create traditions.

Gratitude comes in many forms. During the pandemic, let's expand our focus of thanks to include being grateful for the ability to help others. As we discover the benefits we receive when we put our own needs aside for a moment and reach out to those in need, we begin to experience appreciation in new ways. Often after we have done a favor for someone, they say thank you. We respond with the knee-jerk phrase, "Oh, it's nothing," or a similar deprecating comment. In fact, such statements are untrue. The favor may have meant a great deal more to the recipient than we realize.

Become more aware of the joy you bring others through simple actions. Be grateful that you can give of yourself this way. I once wrote a column about the importance of the phrase "you're welcome." This phrase completes the exchange and is as important as the act of kindness itself. Kindness has tremendous power because it builds trust and leaves us with a good feeling that remains with us forever. Remember the adage, "They may forget what you said, but they will never forget how you made them feel."

Establishing traditions within a family or the larger community requires little more than repeated actions. Why not consider incorporating such actions into your Thanksgiving celebrations? Offering a toast to those who could not be with you is an example of a tradition many families enjoy. Taking turns around the table sharing what each person is grateful for over the past year is another appropriate example. There are so many people whose lives would be transformed if we assumed a level of responsibility equal to their need. Every family is different. Each has unique challenges as well as special talents. Letting others know of our needs is critical to meeting these challenges. Because this can be awkward for various reasons, those of us who are able to must make the time to seek out and help our family, friends, and greater community.

Imagine a world where your neighbors aren't lonely, hungry, or dealing with overwhelming challenges that push them to addiction, violence, and other ways to try to escape their suffering. We can make such a world become a reality if we decide we want to. If making connections with others becomes a higher priority, the healing our society needs so much will take place. If this sounds too good to be true, try doing it anyway. If we follow the suggestion made in the movie *Bill and Ted's Excellent Adventure*, "Be excellent to each other," our eyes will be opened to a whole new kind of Thanksgiving.

# Self-Reflective Exercises

- How do you express gratitude to yourself? If you have done something that makes you feel good about yourself, do you take the time to recognize such feelings? What feelings arise when you are successful?

- How do you express gratitude to others? Do you take some things for granted that you should acknowledge in writing? Can you write a thank-you note in a timely way? If not, why not? What's preventing you from putting pen to paper?

- How do you accept gratitude? Are you aware of your kindness? Do you slough it off as nothing? Be sure to allow others to express their appreciation. Learn to accept it humbly.

- How do you feel when people take you for granted? Do you feel unappreciated, sad, or angry? How do you manage those feelings? Remember that other people's actions often reflect more on their stuff than on yours.

*Pillar 5*

# ENCOURAGEMENT

# Introduction

*All we have to decide is what to do with the*
*time that is given us.*

— J.R.R. Tolkien, *The Fellowship of the Ring*

Encouragement is a fundamental building block of any healthy society. Along with awareness, compassion, humility, gratitude, and responsibility, encouragement plays a critical role in our lives. It is like food for our bodies. It connects us and demonstrates that how we treat one another matters. There is no better way to build a healthy and successful personal relationship or maintain a vibrant community or workplace than by encouraging each other.

Positive reinforcement comes in many forms; the spoken word is the most powerful. Simple phrases such as "please" and "thank you" can speak volumes. We learn from early childhood that receiving and delivering encouraging words deeply affects our sense of belonging. Kindergarten is often the first place where we reinforce all six pillars of civility. At this early age, we begin to distinguish between appropriate and inappropriate behavior through words of encouragement. A simple pat on the back or instructive correction helps reinforce the point.

Encouragement is also critical on the sports field. Successful athletic teams usually adopt encouraging words into their mantras. Coaches and team members alike know that any group becomes more powerful than the sum of its parts by working together and encouraging each other. We learn that we lift the whole team's energy and each player's abilities to their best levels by helping each other. We thrive on our home turf because of a concentration of encouragement. The home team advantage, aided by the home crowd's cheers, can encourage even a less skillful team to triumph. Cheerleaders effectively rally the masses to loud applause and boisterous cheers to instill confidence and raise the group's energy.

In relationships, one of the greatest strengths we have is making our partners feel better about themselves. One of the bonuses of encouraging others is the positive effect it has on us. We feel better about ourselves and bolster our self-esteem by observing and expressing approval of others' actions.

By acknowledging that what someone else does makes a difference in our lives, we affect how others spend their day. When we have a great day, we get a lot more accomplished, and we feel exhilarated and worthy. Encouragement is a powerful principle. If it becomes a regular practice of our parents, teachers, and bosses, the effect is fantastic. Studies have shown that children learn better in a supportive atmosphere if they feel good about themselves. Encouraging family, friends, workers, constituents, and anyone in our communities will result in a nurturing, positive, and healthy environment, creating a productive and happy atmosphere.

Without encouragement, there is a tendency toward bullying and other negative behaviors. A toxic, fear-based environment discourages productivity on every level, whether in education, business, or at home. It is vital to recognize disrespectful, harmful behavior and correct it. Awareness of the problems signals the need for changes in any situation that withholds encouragement.

The success of encouragement relies on our parents, teachers, and managers' wisdom and actions. Once praise is given where it is due, where we live and work become places of mutual respect. We maintain our self-worth and acknowledge the value of those around us.

Encouraging someone requires courage. Introverted, antisocial, or shy people may find that stepping outside their protective shell to engage with and encourage others to follow their chosen path causes anxiety. Moving through this anxiety can require quite a lot of courage. Encouragement is the magic that brings meaning to so many lives. Be courageous every day.

# Teach Etiquette Early

*The hardest job kids face today is learning good
manners without seeing any.*

— Fred Astaire

‿𝓸‿

Some people take offense when others don't use napkins,
and wonder if they're merely witnessing a lack of good
manners. Others learned different table manners, resulting in
occasional confusion.

One reader queried, "At one restaurant, a server picked up
my napkin and placed it on my lap before taking my order. Was
this the proper thing to do? It was a rather high-class eating
place, so I assumed this must be done at such establishments,
as it would never happen at our local Pizza Hut. Perhaps you
can set me right as to the dos and don'ts of napkin etiquette. I
hope you don't find my question too trivial."

First, there are no trivial questions when it comes to proper
etiquette. In some high-end restaurants, it is customary for the
server to place your napkin on your lap. My advice is always
to follow the lead of your host or hostess. As soon as everyone
is seated, the host or hostess should unfold and place their napkin on their lap. The guests should follow in turn. If there is no
host, once everyone is seated (even if it's only two people), you
should unfold and place your napkin on your lap. If you don't,

an attentive waiter will likely step in to do it for you. This isn't rude or condescending but rather is a silent service gesture indicating that the meal is underway. It is a way of communicating that the staff is ready to serve you.

Such questions point to the importance of teaching proper etiquette and good manners at an early age. There is nothing complicated or sophisticated about napkin etiquette. Nor are any of the other habits of good behavior cumbersome or tricky. However, they are learned behaviors. No one is born with good manners or bad manners. We develop manners by emulating our parents, caregivers, and schoolteachers.

But what if our parents never learned proper etiquette or practiced good manners? Sadly, we are often left to learn through trial and error, which can result in awkward life lessons. Why didn't we get the job? Why didn't we get the promotion we were expecting? Important interviews often occur over lunch or dinner, not because the interviewer is worried that you may be hungry, but because they are checking out your necessary life skills. If you don't know how to eat a meal properly, they might wonder what other simple skills you could be lacking. Poor manners are also known as the silent career killer. Sadly, no one will tell you this is the reason you didn't get the job or promotion.

What's even more telling is that you feel uncomfortable at formal meals or at corporate social gatherings where the purpose is to meet clients, mingle, and discuss business. A person without the confidence instilled by knowing proper etiquette will inevitably be at a disadvantage. Take the time to learn good manners and realize the difference having them makes in social and business gatherings.

It is never too late to learn the necessary social graces and corporate etiquette you need to know to feel comfortable and confident in any situation. Some consultants teach short seminars. Many books also deal with this subject. As a society, we have hit rock bottom as far as good manners go, in both social and business circles. If we hope to succeed globally, we must make a concerted effort to acquire and improve them. It should begin at home.

Take the time to have family meals around a correctly set dinner table. Learn to have civil discussions around the dinner table. It is okay to disagree, but it is not okay to be disagreeable. Make good manners a priority at home. Although schools teach many essential core values, parents must lead the charge in teaching and instilling good behavior, making today's youth the leaders of tomorrow.

# Graduations

*There is a good reason they call these ceremonies*
*"commencement exercises." Graduation is not the end;*
*it's the beginning.*

— Orrin Hatch

When spring arrives, some people turn their attention to graduation ceremonies and celebratory parties. There are some complicated issues with announcements and invitations. Graduating from high school or college is an accomplishment worthy of high praise. Graduates and their families are justifiably proud and want to let everyone know. They share this joy with relatives and friends who live far away.

Friends and family who live within a comfortable traveling distance are often invited to the ceremony or celebration. Some schools may limit the number of invitations for logistical reasons. In this case, you can insert a small card with the formal announcement that invites people to any private reception, which the graduate's parents often host.

How is this whole thing most efficiently handled? You will need three lists: one for the graduation ceremony, one for the celebratory party, and one for people receiving announcements only. There will be some duplication, so be sure to cross-check the lists. Invitations should come from the students themselves, no matter who physically does the addressing and mailing. Those living nearby should receive their invitations two to three weeks before graduation. People living far away need a month's notice. Make sure the invitations have an RSVP on them. Don't mail the graduation announcements until a week or two after the ceremony.

The invitations and announcements always look more personal if they are hand-addressed. They do not need to be addressed by the graduate, but try to find someone with legible handwriting, much as you would for a wedding invitation or announcement.

There should be no mention of gifts on either the announcement or the invitations. Invitations do not come with a price of admission. But let's face it: certain milestones call for tangible rewards. Graduation is one of them. Most often, cash is the preferred gift and the one that students hope for most. The best way to get this message out is by word of mouth. People have fantastic networking skills. Plant the idea of cash gifts with one or two persons who will likely attend the graduation and reception and ask them to spread the word.

The amount of the monetary gift is entirely arbitrary. It depends on how close a relationship a person has with the student and their financial stability. It is as simple as that.

When I'm asked for suggestions for appropriate graduation gifts, my advice is to give something useful. Money, a gift certificate to a clothing store, or a gift card are popular choices. Monogrammed pen-and-pencil sets are undoubtedly traditional and often come from close relatives. Perhaps there is an heirloom set from a grandparent that might be appreciated. New telecommunication and entertainment devices abound, and I know of no graduate who would not be thrilled to have one.

People usually want useful, practical things. We remember gifts most when they are things we would love to have but would not likely buy for ourselves. I advise selecting items with the graduate's likes in mind. I try to give something that evokes an "Oh, wow!" response and will be genuinely appreciated. Take a few minutes to think about what someone would really like. Phone a parent or sibling of the graduate, if necessary, to get the inside scoop. Making this extra effort shows that you really care about this person and respect their great accomplishment as much as they do.

At the graduation ceremony itself, everyone should take pride in how they look. Make sure your clothes are clean, perfectly pressed, and fit well. I know it is always tempting to want to be original and unique; every generation likes to put its stamp on fashion. For formal occasions, you will do yourself a favor if you resist this temptation. Buy clothes that you will be happy to wear again. That lime-green jacket may not be so useful down the road. A rule of thumb is to wear traditional clothing. Perhaps choose one item that stands out. For example, men can wear a colorful tie or shirt, and women could wear a stylish hat or unique shirt. Have a great time, and revel in the splendor that comes with this important milestone.

A good education is one of the most critical assets we can have, not to mention a right that should be available to everyone. We celebrate these milestones with commencement exercises, proms, graduation parties, and other activities. Grand marches, academic awards, and scholarship ceremonies further punctuate this exciting time. These festivities serve to celebrate milestones and encourage our youth to strive to live productive, fulfilling lives.

# The First Date

*It was our first date, and I asked what his favorite movie is.*
*He asked if I'd judge him, but instead of judging him,*
*I just loved him.*

— Dominic Riccitello

I remember vividly the first time I asked someone to go out on a date. I needed a bit of courage to extend such an invitation. I knew I had a fun evening planned, but I was nervous. I was just 17, and my date was a girl I had known since early childhood. It's incredible how, as adults, we appreciate those things we most feared as children.

Since then, I have come to realize that first dates don't get any easier. We complicate them with anticipation, agendas, and intentions. When asked about first dates, the most burning question, not surprisingly, is about finances. Who pays the tab on the first date? Traditionally, the person who issues the invitation is the one who pays, although sharing the bill on a first date has become a popular option.

However, many first dates are not traditional, and etiquette guidelines should be flexible. Perhaps a first date is simply a get-together for coffee. With increasing frequency, this date is with a member of the same sex or LGBTQ community. And it isn't unusual for a woman to ask a man out for a first date.

My advice on money matters is to resolve them in advance. For regular get-togethers such as coffee or a movie, perhaps alternating who pays is a fair solution. If going out on a dinner date, know before you even make the reservation who will pay the bill. If you decide to split the bill, be sure to let the waiter know before you order.

Not all dates lead to a long-term relationship. Inviting someone out casually to a fun concert or event is a great way to thank them for a past kindness. It is also a great way to strengthen a platonic friendship. Initiating a social outing is a fun way to break out of the workweek. However, be prepared for the occasional disappointment. Schedules do not always jibe. Don't take it personally or request an explanation. When you ask someone to join you, make it clear that they will be your guest. More than likely, they will reciprocate the invitation.

First dates are excellent times to make good impressions. You may even be meeting your date's parents for the first time. Be sure to wear clean clothes appropriate to the venue. Be freshly bathed and coiffed; brush your teeth and use a breath freshener. Don't talk too much about yourself. Find out as much as you can about what your date enjoys doing when not working or going to school. What books do they read, what music do they listen to, what movies do they watch? Steer away from controversial topics such as religion or politics until you know the person well enough to trust them with personal views.

Before long, you will both have decided if you want to further your friendship. Have compassion for yourself and your date if it becomes clear that you are not compatible. Parting on friendly terms eliminates any negative feelings either of you may have. Compassion will be a strength in any ongoing relationship. Be sure to put the other person's feelings ahead of your own. This consideration is a good rule of thumb for first dates and any other first meetings. Treat each other with respect and kindness, and your first date will become a fond memory.

# Cultural Etiquette

*Often, we may even smile or laugh at adversity, but all
people share the same passions. They merely manifest
differently according to one's culture and conditioning.*

— Yasuo Kuwahara

⌒ᘐ⌒

Canada is filled with people from cultures around the world.
Perhaps this is one of its greatest assets. Canada encourages and celebrates homogeneity while honoring individu-
ality and diversity. It has evolved into a leading nation with
enormous power and respect in part because of the new immigrants' many different strengths and talents.

Because of different cultural communities' ability to remain
non-homogenized, questions arise from time to time about
how people from different cultural backgrounds should interact. Is it a when-in-Rome scenario? Who's to say that one
person is more Canadian than the next? Also, different ethnic
groups tend to live within neighborhoods where they enjoy
their shared customs harmoniously and comfortably.

I find different cultural customs fascinating and always look
forward to visiting people from different backgrounds. When
going on such a visit, I make an effort to check to see what
sorts of fundamental differences there are. Learning something
about a different culture shows interest and respect. Doing so
also makes it less likely that I'll make a major faux pas.

In the business arena in North America, cultural boundaries are significantly blurred. However, to establish a successful and lasting business relationship with a foreigner, understanding their way of doing business is essential. Some people like to get right down to business, and arriving even a minute late can spell disaster. Others want to find out about your personal and family life before they feel comfortable enough to conduct business. As businesspeople, we must learn about these differences, respect them, and conduct business accordingly.

If a gift exchange is part of the protocol, consider the appropriateness of specific gifts, such as flowers, edibles, or something more substantial, depending on how much foreign business you anticipate. Knowing how people greet each other, especially post COVID-19, is also essential, be it a handshake, bow, or kisses on each cheek. If you're invited to a dinner, different types of food are likely to be served. If you have an actual food allergy, phone your host ahead of time. If you are reluctant to try new foods, brace yourself and do the best you can. You won't be poisoned and may even discover a fresh taste sensation!

When you invite people to your home who may not be familiar with your lifestyle or customs, try to make everything comfortable. Ensure that your guests are not overwhelmed or embarrassed by a barrage of new experiences. People like learning about different cultures, and when they are in your home, you should feel comfortable sharing your traditions. Explaining one's home culture can often illuminate the differences between cultures and be a fascinating topic of discussion around the dinner table. Being open-minded and interested in the ways other people have lived and learning about customs from around the world is educational. Acquiring this knowledge makes it amazingly easy for you to have conversations with strangers wherever you may go.

Communicating and connecting with people is the key to success. The foundation and sustainability of any healthy society depend on it. Treat moments of sharing experiences with great respect, gratitude, and humility. There are no two better tools than awareness and mindfulness when forming relationships with people from other lands and cultures.

In many ways, the world is becoming smaller day by day. As a result, we can, and do, make a difference to the people we meet. There is also a real opportunity during these interactions to show compassion for others. We can demonstrate it by being patient and by understanding their challenges while maintaining our integrity. We can also have compassion for ourselves. In the end, we are all human beings, all custodians of our planet. Learning about and respecting our differences will go a long way toward creating peace on earth. Give yourself the task of learning about another culture today. It's enriching.

# Can We Raise Polite Children?

*The way we talk to our children becomes their inner voice.*

— Peggy O'Mara

⌣ᵔ⌣

Good manners matter. Fortunately, a growing number of parents are seeking advice on how to raise their children with good manners. Sadly, an entire generation (or more) grew up with overly flexible guidelines and few boundaries; they didn't learn the significance of knowing right from wrong or that actions have consequences. That void makes learning good manners and socially acceptable behavior challenging for their children.

Children are like sponges when it comes to learning, especially from their parents. From the moment they are born, they instinctively trust that their parents will keep them safe and secure. Absolutely nothing escapes their attention. As parents adapt to setting a better example for their children, they also begin to understand their responsibility for their children's upbringing, safety, and actions! Setting a good example begins and ends at home.

It isn't necessary to overthink the process of teaching good manners. Respecting each other is just not that complicated. Learning to understand the Golden Rule and realizing the consequences of our actions teach us many of life's most important lessons. From an early age, children should learn to show respect for their elders. For instance, children need to learn to stand when an adult enters a room; they won't have inherited this as an instinct. Children learn by following their parents' example or instruction.

Teaching table manners can be a daunting task. Parents concentrate on giving directions and instructions to keep children safe, such as how to carefully handle a knife or not to tip back on your chair. But good manners instill confidence and can make it easier to make friends, achieve better grades, and make better choices. Even the chances of gaining acceptance into one's college of choice or getting a good job can be enhanced by having good manners. In time, good or bad manners will become second nature. Remember that good manners matter!

Introductory etiquette instruction should become part of a child's elementary education. It is no secret that schools are short of both time and money, yet relatively little of either is required to set up such a program. Unfortunately, teaching good manners in school is not a high priority. As a result, the faculty deals with bullying and declining academic performances, ultimately leading to a less civil workforce.

Schools should support good manners. But we cannot place the burden of responsibility for teaching our children how to behave appropriately on school faculty. Raising our children is not the teachers' responsibility. Tasking them with that is inappropriate and unfair. Instead, the school setting ought to benefit from students' proper behavior, and schools should rely on parental guidance to teach the basics of ethical conduct and civility.

Parents need to make good manners a high priority. Children must learn these essential life skills at home. Our homes need to provide a supportive and safe environment for our children to thrive and fully develop to their highest potential.

Yes, it is possible to raise well-mannered children. Clear communication, compassion, and a lot of love, respect, and positive feedback will go a long way toward making the whole learning process more effective and pleasant. Consistently setting a good example is our best tool. By bringing the importance of good manners into sharper focus, tomorrow's leaders will emerge with higher self-esteem and respect for themselves and others.

# A Community of Neighbors

*Good neighbors make a huge difference in*
*the quality of life. I agree.*

— Robert Fulghum

⸺ ৵ ⸺

Most of us live in communities. We regularly engage with others in our community. Who our neighbors are is dictated more by chance than by choice. Fortunately, we need to connect with other people to lead fulfilling lives. We work, play, commune, shop, and generally live our lives connecting with and depending upon those around us. As we spend more time with our neighbors, we often develop relationships, and our lives become enriched.

Since we cannot control who our neighbors are, we never know if they will become lifelong friends. Will they become a source of constant irritation or be just plain good folks with whom we share a pleasant, civil coexistence?

Property maps have clear lines delineating one parcel of land from another. In real life, however, a shared boundary takes on a life of its own. Take, for example, the shared driveway, walkway, hallway, or lawn. I would automatically cut a swath of my neighbor's yard while cutting my own. The same holds true when shoveling snow or sweeping the sidewalk we share. For neighbors who find this kindness awkward or are overtly territorial, respecting their space by keeping a fair distance makes better sense. Although reaching out to such tightly wrapped people can sometimes soften them up, it means investing some time and effort. How important is being a good neighbor?

Respecting neighbors by keeping noise to a reasonable level is polite and, ideally, reciprocated. There are usually noise ordinances that define the hours for loud music, lawn mowers, and power equipment. Common sense should also go a long way toward making good neighbors. Being up front with them in a calm voice and smiling are the most successful ways to approach them if something comes up. Clear communication helps establish peaceful coexistence.

You can also show respect by inviting your neighbors to a get-together, such as a pool party or barbecue or late-night graduation or birthday celebration. Giving your neighbors a heads-up if you're planning a noisy evening is a kind and thoughtful way to show your respect for their airspace. Ideally, when the time comes, they will respect yours as well.

In the unlikely event that there is an actual breach of community peace, whether it's a barking dog, peculiar human traffic patterns, or anything alarming, check with your neighbors before notifying the authorities. Petty crimes often go unnoticed without our neighbors' watchful eyes. Acts of vandalism are examples of behaviors property owners often fail to witness. Good neighbors look out for each other. That's what builds better communities.

# And Like a Good Neighbor

*We all have neighbors. Greet them on the sidewalk or in*
*the elevator but try not to peer through their windows.*
*Windows are to look out from, not into.*

— Alexandra Stoddard

I remember as a small child riding my bicycle or skateboard around my neighborhood without realizing how much I was observing. Over time, subconsciously, I grew to know the routines of dozens of households. I knew when they mowed their lawns, when and where they walked their dogs, and when they entertained friends and family or were away on vacation. Making a mental note of when everything is right with the world gives us a sense of safety and security. Over time, we know what to expect and, more importantly, when something isn't quite right.

As children, we spend our time playing, eating, and sleeping. When we grow up, our lives take on different meanings and additional responsibilities. We no longer have the time to cruise the neighborhood to see who's up to what. However, to maintain our sense of safety and security, we need to realize just how important having a look around can be.

Signs that things are not quite right are newspapers piling up outside a neighbor's front door or long grass growing where a perfectly manicured lawn once grew. When you see these irregularities, take the initiative to either knock on their door or call the authorities.

The size and demographics of a neighborhood determine just how involved people become in others' lives. In communities where there are many children, some parents form associations where shared neighborhood patrols help ensure safety. Safety protocols include observing loitering and looking out for vandalism and anything else out of the ordinary. When something seems suspicious, summon the authorities. They will take whatever actions are needed to return things to normal. It makes sense for private citizens to become familiar with how to protect children from kidnapping, bullying, and many other dangers.

In communities populated by senior citizens, similar measures are equally important. Transportation and health issues, proper nutrition and hygiene, and depression and loneliness are common daily challenges that our neighbors encounter. Keeping an eye out for each other is neighborly.

Safety is paramount. If we believe in strengthening the weakest link first, we must have our priorities in order. Sadly, this rarely happens today; the most vulnerable among us suffer far too much.

As an example, the U.S. Department of Agriculture estimated that more than 11 million children in the United States lived in food-insecure households as of 2018. That means that one in six children may not have consistent access to enough food for an active, healthy life.

Another example is that many men ignore the fact that hitting someone, especially one's spouse, domestic partner, child, or pet, is illegal. We need to reconsider how we, as a society, address these critical issues. Only then can we successfully tackle the challenges of suicide prevention, bullying, domestic violence, illiteracy, and abject poverty.

We cannot rely solely on the slowly turning wheels of government to address these issues. We must take responsibility for protecting and improving our communities and appreciating any available government assistance. Proactive civic associations show leadership in many towns and accomplish much good. We can do more and must never give up.

We need to educate our children about what living in a community is all about. They must learn to be aware of how they interact with others and the effect of such interactions. We need to understand the difference between being nosy and being responsible. Helping neighbors who are in need is part of our civic duty. Following the Golden Rule leads to healthier, stronger neighborhoods and communities.

# What Can We Learn About Good Manners During COVID-19?

*There is more need than ever to rebuild in a just and resilient manner.*

— Madanmohan Rao

N o one will escape the grip of COVID-19. As evidenced by the desperate pleas for help of all kinds, including finances, security, and significantly scaled-up testing, we are experiencing a "novel" type of fear. We look forward to press briefings, but too often, they provide insufficient information, especially around testing, to ease our minds. As a result, we ruminate on the challenges we face and worry about even greater ones that are imminent threats to our safety. The further we fall down the rabbit hole of fear, the faster good manners beat a quick retreat.

We might find ourselves reacting to our daily routines with unkindness. We need to reflect on how we feel and how our feelings affect us and those around us. How we treat others is an excellent barometer of how balanced we are within our own lives. Maintaining balance makes a significant difference in how we experience life. As responsible members of our households, we benefit from our connections to each other. Acts of kindness reinforce the concern we have for others, and we must always be kind. Kindness behaves like a boomerang. Whatever goodness we put out into the world will always return.

The interdependency on which we thrive depends on civil discourse, acts of kindness, and compassion. During these stressful times, our elected officials must level with us; they must share all the facts and answer our questions to our complete satisfaction. Some will argue that this is impossible because there is so much we simply do not know. After all, we are in uncharted territory. This lack of knowledge is the apparent inconvenient truth. However, communication is crucial, and if constituents do not feel more secure after press briefings, the conversations must improve. No one wins when we abandon transparency and clarity.

Within our homes, we have many opportunities to refine our relationships. We soon appreciate the value of our own space, complete with the boundaries we lay down around it. We respect others' space more readily, too, as we live on a new schedule imposed upon us by COVID-19.

Creating a daily routine can help alleviate tensions and imbalances in our newly found close quarters. Allowing others to experience their feelings and express their emotions is another way to support each other through these rough seas. All of our feelings are valid, and we should not dismiss them.

Although we are unable to change our current circumstances, we can show compassion for each other. No two people will experience this powerful jolt to our senses in precisely the same way. Compassion removes any judgment, and humility eliminates any need to judge in the first place. Our anxiety levels rise when we feel we are under the microscope, so practicing empathy and compassion with everyone helps calm the waters.

Within our temporary permanent hangout, we can also use our newfound spare time to learn a new skill. Now might be the perfect chance to begin a yoga practice, learn to meditate, or conquer your fears of baking. Reading can also help transport us from our current situation, if only for a few moments. Writing provides some of us with a way to share our innermost thoughts, if only with ourselves. Sharing our ideas with our family over a home-cooked meal can happen more easily while sheltering at home. Let's relish these times together. Of course, we wish our lives would return to the old normal as quickly as possible, but our memories of these times of upheaval can be good ones if we make the conscious choice to make them so.

Good manners are not going out of style as a result of COVID-19. Some practices may change, but the principle behind them won't. Greetings may well gravitate away from the handshake and shift to something such as bowing the head— as long as it's not a fist bump! We may find ourselves seated farther apart at the dinner table, but the same dining manners apply. Hats will never have a rightful place at the dinner table (or on it!).

Because good manners reflect common sense and the Golden Rule, COVID-19 should not affect them. Good manners are about putting the other person first and making them feel welcome and at ease. In these tumultuous times, I reiterate the importance of supporting our elected officials' decisions and actions. They are working on our behalf to keep us safe: that's their job. It is also their job to encourage us through clear communication.

# Be Sure to Be Present

*Focus on opportunities, not setbacks. Focus on what you
can do, not what you can't. Focus on the present moment,
not the past or the future. Empower yourself.*

— Akiroq Brost

H ave you ever noticed how you'll hear a phrase in such a way that you do a double take and think seriously about what you just heard? This happened to me on February 3, 2021, just before Congressman Pete Buttigieg's swearing-in as transportation secretary, when it was reported that Vice President Kamala Harris offered, "Be sure to be present. It will go by quickly."

I immediately thought what a kind gesture this was. Although the two politicians have a great deal of experience, the compassion offered at that moment reverberated around the world. The idea of being fully present is common today. Many philosophers and New Agers have long espoused the importance of this view of mindfulness. It appears that achieving this goal is as elusive now as it ever has been.

What I also heard reported was Mr. Buttigieg's response. He said, "Thank you." He knew how important this moment would be for him, and he appreciated the reminder. We can spend so much time wrapped up in the emotion of the moment, the logistics of where to stand, and in not forgetting our responsibilities, that we forget to savor and enjoy the moment for what it truly represents. Although this simple exchange between Harris and Buttigieg did not garner headlines, it is one of the most poignant pieces of advice one leader can give to another.

There is a distinction between the formal, legal, historical process and its sheer personal enjoyment. We reach milestones that zoom by us in the blink of an eye. These events and accomplishments often require considerable preparation and planning. After all, we spend years attending school to graduate. Planning a wedding can take weeks, if not longer. Promotions at work, welcoming home newborns, and developing new friendships all qualify as significant life events. As we look back over the years, how many of these moments do we readily recall so we can relive the joy we experienced?

Our most memorable events are those that had the most significant emotional effect. The reason they were so powerful is most likely because they captured our undivided attention. We may not remember the details of the day, their formal, legal, historical parts, but we remember how they made us feel. Unfortunately, the most stressful times in our lives can affect us the most deeply. Because those times commandeer our fight-or-flight instincts, they are far more necessary to our survival and therefore capture our attention more easily.

The parts of our lives that bring relaxation, pleasure, and peace tend to arrive quietly. They do not require the same heightened attention as stressful moments. Too often, they come and go with little fanfare. How unfair it seems that our most pleasant memories occupy so much less of our mind than our most stressful. That is, nonetheless, the way our minds operate. Therefore, it is all the more important to remind ourselves to be present during the fun times.

In times such as the COVID-19 pandemic, many of us live in a constant state of fear. Despite explanations from our elected officials intended to guide and comfort us, most of us are struggling, and many of us are suffering. For those of us who find coping with today's challenges overwhelming, finding moments of pleasure is more complicated than ever. Our lives are upside down. Our daily routines are no longer routines, but rather movable goalposts riddled with desperation, fear, and anger. We feel like our rights and freedoms no longer exist, with no light in sight.

There is a light at the end of the tunnel, however. We have each other for encouragement and support through these unsettled times. We have our human spirit, which we can employ to uplift ourselves and others when feeling unheard, depressed, or hopeless. When we feel able to help someone who is suffering, we must do so. If we can feed a hungry person, we must provide for them. We may find those less fortunate who cannot navigate the "system." We can be the connectors for these folks by putting them in touch with programs that can help or with their elected officials.

Above all, we must take our turn at reminding ourselves to be present, because this will go by quickly. By focusing on our many blessings, the milestones we reach, and our trusted friends, we can become mindful of the details we often overlook. We can savor the moments of joy, victory, and accomplishment as we so deserve to do.

Those of you in leadership roles must focus on encouraging others through your words and actions. Too often we forget how meaningful words of encouragement can be. Such expressions can raise our spirits, help us create beautiful memories, and even save lives.

# Why Encouragement?

*A word of encouragement during a failure is worth more*
*than an hour of praise after success.*

— Unknown

~⌇~

A s human beings, our brains are wired to give and receive encouragement primarily for our survival and perpetuation. Actions as fundamental as suckling, eating, and walking are habits parents foster in their children from the moment they are born. Unfortunately, in our time-starved, fear-laden society, we expect our children to learn these basic skills easily and quickly. Curiously enough, when kids stumble, many parents lose patience and replace the carrot with the stick. This unfortunate default confuses a young mind, creating fear and hesitancy with each ensuing step. On the other hand, encouragement provides the necessary support and sense of safety and security that reduces the anxiety that can come from learning new things.

Most of us enjoy watching Olympic athletes go for the gold. We love rooting for our favorite athletes, sitting on the edge of our seats as world records fall and new champions are crowned. As we listen to the sportscaster's commentary, we hear moving backstories that illustrate the extraordinary dedication, sacrifice, and hard work of these athletes striving to become the best they can be. The encouragement of their coaches, parents, and many other supporters is important to their success.

As an audience, we relish the triumphs, sometimes imagining that someday that could be us. We instinctively recognize excellence. While watching the athletes compete, we notice coaches offering a hug and words of encouragement after each performance, whether it was a gold medal showing or not, which ensures that they maintain their competitive spirit as they carry on, acknowledging that they did their best.

One of the most poignant memories of the 2020 Olympics was the sudden and unexpected withdrawal from the gymnastics competition of Simone Biles, the most decorated gymnast of all time. As accustomed as she was to years of competition and the myriad physical, mental, and emotional challenges of high-level sports, she reached her breaking point. She thankfully had the good sense to know what was best for her and to follow her instincts. Despite the media's focus on her decision for the team's good, her challenge was personal. Fortunately, the world embraced her decision. As a result, the much-needed attention cast on the world of mental health deserves a gold medal of its own.

Few of us become world-class competitors. However, all of us face world-class challenges of our own, and we compete in our own form of Olympics throughout our lives. Unfortunately, most of us don't have professional coaches tasked with bringing out our best. Instead, too many of us face taskmasters who are usually interested in their best interests, not ours.

This dynamic fails more times than not. Within our families and workplaces, criticism has replaced encouragement, to the detriment of all of us. Unfortunately, most of us don't realize the damage we inflict when we lose our patience or, even worse, our tempers.

The way to restore a more positive focus in our lives is through empathy. Above all else, empathy requires our attention and time, two commodities we often find in short supply. By initially examining our personal relationship with empathy and encouragement, we can begin to understand how we interact with others, especially those who depend on us: our children, students, and employees. Do we have the patience to help someone who is struggling? If not, is our response to their struggle helpful, or does it serve only to further their pain?

When people entrust us with any part of their lives, our responsibility is to respect that trust with compassion and humility. To be empathetic, we must put ourselves in another person's shoes. In so doing, one question that may be helpful to ask is what matters to them, more so than what's the matter. This simple distinction places the focus of our concern on them and not on the issue.

Whether our role is to encourage or be encouraged, we need to be aware of how we affect others and how they affect us. We also need to have compassion, accepting that we all struggle even while doing the best we can. Humility will remind us that there are no big shots and that on most levels our problems are no different from anyone else's. Gratitude allows us to accept help with an open heart, knowing that we will return the favor one day. And finally, as community members, we need to recognize our responsibility to help others who need our support. Remember that a rising tide lifts all boats. So when we help one, we help all.

Those of us who didn't receive the encouragement we deserved got the short stick. As we become role models through our service to others, we need to eliminate the short sticks and replace them with carrots.

# *Self-Reflective Exercises*

- How do you encourage yourself to do better or reduce your suffering? How does this make you feel?

- How do you encourage others to do better? Does helping others affect you?

- Do you encourage yourself and others whenever possible? Such possibilities abound.

- When someone encourages you to try something new, what is your first reaction? Are you comfortable with that first response? If not, what do you do, and how does such reconsideration make you feel?

*Pillar 6*

# RESPONSIBILITY

# Introduction

*Take responsibility for your own happiness;*
*never put it in other people's hands.*

— Roy T. Bennett

⌒‿◞‿⌒

We spend our lives learning to discern our responsibilities from those of others and from those that belong in the realm of our higher power. Taking full responsibility for our words and actions is critical. When we all shirk our responsibilities, chaos ensues.

Have you ever noticed how often people fail to take responsibility for their actions but rarely hesitate to let other people know when they forget theirs? We all fall into this trap from time to time. We rationalize it by saying that we care about the other person and don't want them to make the same mistakes we've made or that we helped them save time or money. The fact of the matter is that these challenges are not ours: they are theirs. Just as we learned from making our mistakes, they must be allowed to learn from theirs.

As adults our first responsibility is the safety and well-being of our children. This duty includes how we conduct ourselves around them, how we relate to them emotionally, and how we teach them to be responsible community members.

Parents often give children some responsibility for helping around the house. Sometimes they reward them for these chores with a weekly allowance, but not always, as the children could merely be expected to pull their weight. We learn how others rely on us to do stuff, how to be responsible, and how to keep up our end of the bargain.

In concert with other pillars, we need to examine our motives for intruding into someone else's life and have compassion for ourselves for doing so. Our intrusions usually come with an unhealthy dose of judgment. Are we being helpful or are we just being nosy, judgmental, and controlling? Are we bullying them into adopting our path, denying them the right to follow their own?

What happens to us when we do not take responsibility for our actions or are unwilling to accept the consequences? How often do we blame others for our unfortunate situations? This refusal to own up and face the music can deteriorate into living a life of fear, dishonesty, and incivility.

No matter how we view any action that causes us undue stress or suffering, we always share some responsibility for both the situation and the pain. Once we decide to take full responsibility for our lives, we have all the power necessary to make any desired changes. When we blame others, we give away our control, which results in them suddenly holding sway over us. Understanding this dynamic allows us to solve problems more gracefully and to move away from suffering.

When we see ourselves beginning to take responsibility for someone else's suffering, we need to remember to step back.

As much as we want to help others, it is inappropriate to make their choices for them. Their choices rest solely with them. We can still help by having compassion, giving encouragement, or lending a hand. Nevertheless, we must respect other people by not trampling on their boundaries and inserting ourselves into their lives without permission.

When we distinguish between when to help and when not to help, we can take appropriate responsibility in any situation. We developed this ability during childhood and adolescence. This ability is one of the greatest gifts we can give our children or those we care for. This ability to discern seems like a simple enough matter. Still, too often, we don't place a high enough priority on it.

Whether at home or work, have a clear understanding of the importance of this pillar of responsibility. It will affect your success, your level of happiness, and the mutual respect we crave so strongly.

# Civility Begins at Home

*Teaching civility is an obligation of the family.*

— Stephen Carter

⸻

Civility must begin at home. It is our responsibility. Only from there can it connect with all of life's arenas. Without civility at home, we have little left but to try to cope in a fearful society. Treating everyone and every living thing with respect and compassion is what civility is all about. Our behavior is also a crystal-clear mirror reflecting our true self, including our deeper inner self. We are occasionally not even civil with ourselves. Protecting our borders, cultures, and values by excluding all others is poisoning our society's very fabric. This dynamic is not solely an American phenomenon but appears throughout the world.

I listened to a broadcaster on NPR explain that one of our "esteemed" elected officials declared there is no place in politics for civility. To my way of thinking, politics is the one place where civility is most needed. The politics I grew up with afforded a platform where healthy debates could take place. Where have all the diplomats gone? The days of choosing between two or more people of integrity in an election have disappeared. Why is it that people with differing opinions cannot debate without treating each other with disdain? Is it not possible to disagree about a matter without being disagreeable?

Our elected officials are our political leaders. They enjoy all kinds of privileges. Yet they display such rude behavior with their colleagues that one must wonder whether they are even capable of conducting the nation's business. These are the people we still hold in high esteem. I wonder why.

What's more puzzling is that because we hold these so-called leaders in high regard, we justify and normalize their behavior as acceptable. However flawed they are on many levels, their irresponsible behavior further validates and encourages incivility. We unwittingly pass these values on to our children, tomorrow's stewards of our fragile planet.

We share a natural, almost palpable need for control over at least some part of our lives. What we have traditionally held as important and worth protecting are our political and religious belief systems. We cling to these more tightly than ever today. I believe it is in part because we live in such a fast-paced world that there is little we can hold on to long enough to achieve that sense of control we so desperately desire.

And our political views: why must we protect them so vigorously? What is it about these beliefs that cause us to raise our voices to make our point clearer? Could we not have the strength of conviction we need to connect our hearts with our heads?

Politicians from both sides of the aisle are equally responsible for the dissolution of civility. Besides, their inappropriate use of language is disparaging, giving a whole new meaning to "politically incorrect." I am unclear about their true intentions, as they likely are as well. Still, the messages carry potent subliminal reminders, implying that anyone who disagrees with them is dangerous.

Political posturing is part of the process of free government. But what has happened to reason? Do politicians honestly believe that their constituents can't make informed decisions after hearing responsible arguments from all sides? Perhaps, as with many things in life, they merely mirror their inabilities and feelings of inadequacy. However, the time has come for all of our elected officials, not just a few, to start acting like leaders. With some practice, who knows, they could even become leaders.

Incivility is irresponsible, plain and simple. Leading by example should show our youth and others how to interact respectfully, but only if we choose to do just that.

# RSVP

*Well, I'll admit I have had to polish myself off once or twice, but yes! When I RSVP to a party, I make it my business to come!*

— Samantha Jones

Most invitations request an RSVP. The translation of RSVP, the French expression *repondez s'il vous plaît*, is simply "please respond" or "please reply." The RSVP is essential for hosts to finalize party or function arrangements. It indicates how many people will or will not attend the event. It informs the host how to proceed with ordering food and beverages, creating a seating plan, hiring the correct number of servers, and other considerations in planning an auspicious occasion.

Most people do reply to private party invitations. Once you accept an invitation, you need to attend the event, especially at a seated meal. If an emergency occurs, simply let the host know as soon as possible, but no-shows are a fast way off the next guest list. Likewise, last-minute RSVPs are annoying.

For public or institutional affairs, it is equally important to reply to invitations promptly. These events require a lot of planning, and a head count is necessary. Some people think RSVP means "regrets only." It does not. When I receive an invitation to an opening at a museum with an RSVP, I call immediately to let them know one way or another if I will attend. No one is exempt from replying. Many times, public figures receive invitations to special events as a sign of respect and courtesy. They must respond to such requests for the same reasons everyone else must.

If you have not replied to the invitation for a large public gathering, do not just show up thinking your host will be thrilled to see you. I have been to events where they keep a list of who has replied: if you're not on that list, you may not be welcome. You are less likely to be turned away at the door for a nonprofit group. Because these organizations cannot afford to offend anyone, the protocol is often broken or stretched. Be prepared for a solicitation for a donation or a request for volunteer help with various projects. These are some of the ways nonprofits survive.

There are various timelines to follow when sending invitations, depending on the event or party. However, one should RSVP within 48 hours of receiving any invitation if possible. If you receive an invitation in the mail, you should reply in writing. When you're asked to reply to a telephone number or email, follow that request. When an invitation contains a reply card, fill out the required information and return it promptly. Once a person RSVPs, the host accepts whatever decision the guest has made. Questioning people who send their regrets is inappropriate.

Invitations are precise. If an invitation is addressed to "Mr. John Doe and Guest," Mr. Doe may escort the guest of his choice. "Mr. and Mrs. John Doe and Family" refers to immediate family, i.e., children. If the invitation does not say "and family," do not ask if you may bring the children or anyone else. Such a request puts the host in an awkward position and is rude. However, in the case of an informal party, such as a pool party, it is acceptable to call and explain that you have houseguests and ask if you may bring them along. More often than not, extra guests are welcome at casual gatherings.

RSVPs are one of the essential parts of an invitation. It is our responsibility to respond promptly, and it is one small way that guests can contribute to the party's success and help ensure less stress for the host. This small gesture is always a winner.

# The Promise

*A promise must never be broken.*

— Alexander Hamilton

⁓

A handshake is as good as a promise. Well, at least it used to be. When I was a young boy, my grandfather explained how business deals in the good old days concluded with a simple handshake, which was as good as a contract. Over time, the integrity of this informal agreement has, sadly, all but disappeared. It is very disheartening for someone with honorable intentions to be painted with the same broad brush as the unscrupulous. In our current culture of fear, people have become skeptical and err on the side of caution: alas, the verbal promise sealed with a handshake is no longer trusted.

There is great importance to teaching our children that keeping promises is the right thing to do. I heard a story about a child who had spent his allowance on a much-coveted toy; then he wanted more money to buy something else. This impatience is not unusual for small children and is their way of exploring boundaries and pushing limits. However, an allowance comes only once a week. This arrangement is a contract of sorts that both parties should respect. It teaches children the meaning of respect and responsibility. If we don't understand this by adolescence, we will likely face some pretty challenging life lessons just when we least expect them.

Sometimes we make promises based more on emotion than on common sense. When we are desperate or under undue stress, we will agree to almost anything. The results can be disastrous. Don't rush into making promises you may later regret.

Most of us believe that a promise is a promise and that breaking one is wrong. Yet we admit to having broken at least one promise somewhere along the way, whether circumstances in our lives changed or we could no longer honor the deal. Compassion and forgiveness can calm the waters here. Still, we put a lot of stock in our ability to keep our word. A broken promise can lead to a broken friendship.

We tend to look up to people who keep their word. There was a time when politicians, media personalities, and sports heroes were our mentors for this very reason. Sadly, this has all changed. We can no longer believe most politicians, we are skeptical of what we hear or read in the media, and sports heroes often disappoint.

Fortunately, we all know people who speak kindly of others, steer clear of exaggeration, and see both sides of a discussion while thoughtfully weighing the pros and cons. These people help us maintain morality and integrity in our lives.

In Don Miguel Ruiz's remarkable book *The Four Agreements*, one of his principles is to be true to your word. This tenet is a foundational building block for any relationship, whether it is personal or professional. Think hard before making a promise. It's a big deal and carries great responsibility. If we are not responsible for what we say, our credibility evaporates, and our relationships may deteriorate. One's word is one's honor.

# Holiday Obligations

*When our relatives are at home, we have to think of all their good points, or it would be impossible to endure them.*

— George Bernard Shaw

⌒

During the holidays, some people find themselves in the same quandary year after year. Do we drive to celebrate with our family, or do we invite them to visit us for a change? New challenges arose during the COVID-19 crisis. Staying in touch with our loved ones meant clearing new hurdles. But taking the time to connect is particularly important now. The epidemic of loneliness has a tight hold on many people who live by themselves or cannot visit their families for any number of reasons.

Many of us find it challenging to juggle our holiday obligations. The more our families and extended families expand, the more complicated these schedules become. When I was young, our routines defined our holiday traditions and never changed: we knew what to do at the scheduled time. As I grew older and my world expanded, I learned to share my time evenly.

We want everyone to be happy during the holidays and to feel like they are the most special person in the world. From a practical and logistical viewpoint, this is not always possible.

A rule of thumb is that those family members who are most senior in age deserve the most consideration for many reasons. Older people don't travel as readily as they once did; they may find it more comfortable and pleasant to have you call or visit them during the holidays.

Married couples must decide which in-laws they want to spend time with. Many have no choice but to drive from family to family, no matter the weather conditions. Juggling can be trying, but it is often the best solution. Holiday festivities carry many traditions that families enjoy sharing and passing on to their children and grandchildren. These traditions help define a healthy society; facilitating them within a family is a good thing.

The holidays are also a time to create your own traditions. Pick a day during the season to spend with your immediate family. Decide to cook a special meal or open a gift. Decorations can be put up and removed at your discretion. I have a friend who keeps a few Christmas items around her house all year long. It's all up to you.

I can think of no better time of year than the holidays to embrace etiquette's number one cardinal rule: put others first whenever possible. If we take the time to consider what is best for others, we may be surprised at how easy it is to be accommodating. The adage "It is more blessed to give than to receive" became an adage because it is true.

# Handling Unprofessional Professionals

*Leadership is never an avenue to be self-serving but a
platform to render great service to people.*

— Ifeanyi Enoch Onuoha

⸻

People become riled about doctors, waitstaff, bankers, shop-
keepers, and hotel managers, not to mention call center
telephone operators.

Incompetence is an unavoidable part of any professional
landscape. Many people hang out their shingles, claiming to be
authorities about one thing or another, without realizing the responsibility of doling out advice on any number of topics. Di-
plomas and certificates may cover their office walls, but this is
mere window dressing and may have little to do with credibility.

Unprofessional behavior from people we trust throws us off
guard. The difficulty is deciding how to respond to these "up-
ended apple carts" in an appropriate way. A levelheaded approach is the best way to navigate these unpleasant waters and
move forward.

One friend recently described a visit to a gerontologist's office to understand when the early stages of dementia might be
present with a loved one. He was justifiably puzzled when told,

"Unless the person can no longer make French toast or control their bodily functions, there is nothing to worry about." When trying to glean information of a critical and personal nature, like this concern about dementia, diligence is necessary. Even though unprofessional answers are often dismissive, insensitive, and confusing, we still need to carry on. Family members know when behaviors change in a loved one more accurately than a physician who has never met them. In this case, the professional wasn't helpful, and it would have been appropriate to thank them for their time and go back to the referring doctor for another suggestion.

Nothing is more frustrating than interacting with uncaring professionals in situations calling for specific skills and awareness. Take, for example, a server who has little or no knowledge of food preparation or wine suggestions. This information does not fall out of the sky. If they lack this experience, it is not their fault. Not all servers receive the adequate training they need to do their job well. Customer service is not always as strong as it should be in every restaurant. Many servers have no idea how to address a customer properly, let alone an entire table. Training staff is the responsibility of the restaurant owner. Forcing an employee into service without adequate training is foolhardy, unfair, and irresponsible.

Shop clerks who pay no attention to you when you enter their store are another source of irritation. I fully understand if they are busy with other customers; however, chatting on a cell phone, texting, or even reading a book or filing their nails is annoying and irresponsible. Learning to greet customers civilly is not a new concept, but it seems foreign in today's time-precious world.

Dealing with banks can be equally frustrating. We all know that banks are necessary, but they can also be a source of frustration. New banking policies, stacked bank fees, and unexplainable delays in completing transactions can be understandably irritating. Consider yourself lucky when bank personnel take the time and interest to solve your problem satisfactorily. Although this responsibility rests clearly with the bank's management, our patience usually proves to be our greatest asset.

Maintaining our composure during these annoying times can be a challenge. Ending our agitation as quickly as possible requires exercising emotional intelligence. Having this ability shows our compassion. In many cases, we can serve as mentors to avoid similar future situations and reflect on why these irritants have such power over us by taking responsibility for our upset.

In all of these examples, the commonsense bottom line is that responsibility for our health, enjoyment, and state of mind rests primarily with us. How we choose to react to surprises, whether they manifest as unprofessionalism or some other unnecessary stress, indicates how grounded, centered, and civil we are. A solution rarely requires raising one's voice, stomping about like a small child, or bullying someone. Taking Granny's advice and counting to 10 before speaking can work wonders. Oh, and throw in a smile for good measure.

# The Online Breakup

*Sometimes it takes a heartbreak to shake us awake
and help us see we are worth so much more than
we're settling for.*

— Mandy Hale

Imagine receiving a text message from someone you have been dating for a few weeks, telling you they are too busy to continue seeing you. Life has just become too complicated for them to maintain a relationship. How would that make you feel?

You may be thinking this would never happen to you. Oddly enough, however, it happens all the time, and at an increasingly alarming rate. Some people now consider this mode of communicating sensitive personal matters perfectly acceptable. I am here to tell you that it is unacceptable and irresponsible; it is also disrespectful, cowardly, and insensitive.

Face-to-face communication is the best way to discuss concerns of a personal nature. Cowards hide behind technology and social media's protective wall to escape reality and deaden the pain that challenging moments produce. Sticking your head in the sand and hoping the day's problems will disappear is a convenient and painless (albeit temporary) way to handle unpleasantness. However, we all eventually come to realize that this is not a permanent solution. You simply cannot achieve the same closure using such an impersonal approach. The courage required seems impossible to muster at times, but we will reach a solution far more gracefully if we persevere.

Relationships cover a full spectrum of emotional connections. Some are very casual and don't involve any real commitment other than respect and compassion. Others require a lifetime commitment, where a blending of souls occurs and lives become inseparably entwined. Somewhere in this broad spectrum fall all of the relationships we form throughout our lives.

When we become emotionally involved with someone, we deepen our connection with that person. We need to be aware of our interpersonal relationships and to value them. After all, without interaction with friends, we would not thrive or even survive. Friendships can last a lifetime and enrich our lives.

However, if things head south, ending a relationship can carry real danger. Not all breakups end peacefully. Be sure to bring a friend along if you have concerns about your safety. Should drugs, alcohol, or violence be part of the equation, use common sense and seek help. There are resources available to everyone. Calling 911 is sometimes a very sensible place to begin. If you are in a bad relationship, get out of it. This principle applies to both personal and professional relationships. Safety is always number one!

For a variety of reasons, friendships can and do change over time. Everything changes. Knowing where we stand with each other gives us security in our daily lives. Not knowing where we stand leads to anxiety and self-doubt, sometimes even to fear and anger. If you need to end a relationship, be sure to consider the other person's feelings. Because they too have invested their trust and vulnerability, it is helpful to know how they might react to the relationship's changing or ending. Considering another's feelings acknowledges them with compassion.

As convenient as the Internet has become for most of us, using it to break up a romantic relationship in such an impersonal way is cowardly and disrespectful. Life continually provides challenges. People get together, and people break up. It happens all the time, and it is very healthy. You can face the music with courage and find time to sit down with your partner and explain how you feel and why you need a change. Take full responsibility for your feelings without blaming anyone else, and you will find a resolution.

# The Cell Phone Intruder

*Go without the latest iPhone, explore the*
*world and discover.*

— El Fuego

⌒

Selfish, boorish behavior has become the norm rather than
the exception for how many people behave in public. People appear so rushed, so self-absorbed, and so inconsiderate
that they seem to live in another world.

On the train from Moncton to Montreal, a friend endured
listening to two people chattering away on their cell phones.
Both were irritating. The young woman swore profusely and
complained about not having had a smoke in forever. The older woman was four wines in and talked for four hours straight
between relentless hiccupping and giggling.

Whose responsibility is it to inform people on a train that
they should not be on their cell phones having loud, casual
conversations? Perhaps the transit company could accommodate these people by providing an alternative area to have their
discussions.

Having never had the pleasure of riding the great Canadian
rails, I will trust that either there were no rules or they weren't
being enforced. Both Britain and the United States designate

some railcars as "quiet cars." Here you may not use your cell phone for lengthy conversations and certainly not for loud ones. You may not even chat with your fellow passengers.

You are well within your rights to quietly and privately address the issue with the offending party(ies). Otherwise, you are merely being complicit. As with any situation where someone is infringing on your airspace, you can certainly speak up. Whether they react badly to being told how rude they are or not, disrespecting people's boundaries is wrong. Calling them out is appropriate!

Some of us are more generous than others when it comes to giving people the benefit of the doubt. After all, everyone has emergencies and challenging days. However, obnoxious behavior is never justified. People who are in despair or out of sorts should make an effort to seek solace with friends and family privately. Airing your dirty laundry on the train, or discussing personal health problems, boss problems, mate problems, and so on in a public forum is never appropriate. When people feel overwhelmed, they become fearful and defensive. Broadcasting their issues loudly and publicly somehow makes them feel better. These folks need our compassion more than our condemnation. Still, we do need to call them out for their unacceptable behavior.

Whether on trains, planes, or automobiles, respecting the space you share with others is essential and responsible. Just because other people behave in an uncivil manner does not mean you can. This backsliding of respect for others, this utter disregard for how you affect other people, and this reckless, bullying behavior need to stop. Somewhere along the line, someone's parents simply forgot to say "No."

Yes, we need to teach children about the appropriate use of cell phones in public when they receive their first phones. But it is up to us to protect our boundaries and comfort zones. Just be sure not to be rude about it!

# Obligations and Responsibilities

*You may believe that you are responsible for what you
do, but not for what you think. The truth is that you are
responsible for what you think because it is only at this
level that you can exercise choice. What you do comes
from what you think.*

— Marianne Williamson

⌇

I once addressed a small group of people at a political gathering. The focus was on how important it is to roll up your
sleeves and get involved in the election process.

We all have unique perspectives on life based on our lived
experience, knowing what we like and dislike, what we aspire
to, and who we respect and use as mentors. But do we have
the awareness and knowledge to choose the political candidate
who will best represent our perspective?

Sadly, many of us find politics to be unsavory, confusing,
or irrelevant. As a result, we don't get involved enough even
to understand the various platforms. We don't think our voice
matters. We don't think our vote counts. We make our way
through the world despite who is in office.

Divisiveness, foolhardiness, and confusion dominate today's politics. This dynamic should cause us to take a greater
interest in our elected officials' performance. They need to be

held accountable, given the tremendous amount of power they hold. The not-so-quiet revolution that has been taking place is not going away. We live in a culture of fear. Discussing the obligations and responsibilities we face is critical. We need to step out of the shadows and assert ourselves bravely. It is our right to do so, because we live in a free world.

Obligations and responsibilities differ in that an obligation is often something we must do that originates from outside of us. Responsibilities arise from within us.

Obligations fall primarily in the laps of our elected officials. Running the government comes with all sorts of rules, regulations, and guidelines that are generally inflexible by design although not written in stone. Government jobs have both definition and flexibility. How elected officials choose to execute their duties is their responsibility. Herein lies the political theatrics characterizing different parties: their values and their tactics.

Although civility should be the order of the day for elected officials, who have historically been people we looked up to and emulated, this is no longer the case. A general lack of solid leadership has nurtured a culture of fear that threatens to overtake much of the free world. We have lost the ability to have civil discourse and debate essential matters. Some have even lost interest in accepting the results after an election. These are indicators that trust has dangerously eroded in society. This ugly truth is evident in government, the workplace, our communities, and even our own families.

To bring civility back with trust and respect, we must become more aware of what is going on in our families, communities, workplaces, and government. To develop a keener awareness, we must pay closer attention to what other people are doing and listen more carefully to what they say. By taking these two actions, you can think about and begin to understand multiple perspectives. These are also the best ways to strengthen your point of view.

With this greater awareness, our responsibility is to decide how we can be the best stewards of the planet. That role is the one common denominator that binds humans together. We cherish the family unit as a nurturing core group, and we can expand this concept into our communities, making them safe and vibrant. When we encourage civility in the workplace, new opportunities to understand the significance of emotional intelligence can develop, resulting in a psychologically healthy environment, which should be a top priority.

# Speaking Truth to Power During COVID-19

*These days, a sling of truth still can make Goliath fall.*

— Tom Althouse

⌒

Civility is on tenterhooks as we struggle to cope with the challenges COVID-19 continues hurling at us. Many of us are experiencing stress in ways we never before imagined. Our fight-or-flight alert systems are working overtime as we navigate these fear-filled days.

Living in a state of constant fear does not lend itself to being civil. It has the opposite effect. Unfortunately, moving from a state of fear to one of calm is easier said than done. Unless we have an accessible working knowledge of meditation or breathing techniques, or practice yoga routinely, we will not be able to break the bonds of fear by ourselves. We will need encouragement and support from our friends, family, and coworkers.

Herein lies the rub. The facts reveal that in non-COVID times, 25 percent of us lived with a mental illness or disability. Estimates vary, but during the pandemic, this number is likely significantly higher. Additionally, statistics consistently show that about 67 percent of people in the workforce do not like their jobs because they cannot depend on their coworkers or bosses when problems arise. And on top of this, we are all facing significant changes in our daily routines, which renders us far less able to provide the support and encouragement needed.

Before March 2020, we were aware that many systems within the government needed an overhaul. Ironically, these systems were the ones most affected by the pandemic. The new challenges facing the departments of education and health as well as the Royal Canadian Mounted Police are overwhelming. We need more teachers, nurses, doctors, and other frontline workers, including police officers and firefighters, to meet society's growing demands.

This situation causes short-term reactionary thinking to replace long-term proactive planning. Since leaders are especially subject to this dynamic in the workplace, including within the government, employees bringing a matter to their attention risk retribution. Although this risk has always been a factor in speaking truth to power, the pandemic exacerbates it.

Holding on to power and control is nothing new. This need is at the very root of the grave lack of equality and inclusion we currently endure. The fear of giving up any power causes leaders to retreat from such virtues as humility, compassion, and responsibility. As a result, most of us are denied our fundamental rights as outlined in the International Covenant on Civil and Political Rights, which Canada, along with other countries, ratified in 1976. Denying all people these rights eats away at our democratic form of government and the civility on which it is based.

Speaking truth to power often carries high risk. If as a society we are to heal from the current upheaval, we need to regain civility by respecting one another. One way to accomplish that is by answering legitimate questions as they arise. If that does not occur, it usually indicates one of three problems: deception, cover-up, or incompetence. The lack of transparency frustrates each of us differently. We all have different perspectives and different concerns. These stressful matters evoke fear. Furthermore, they are dismissive, disrespectful, and unfair.

The remedy for this can be found only in a strategic change of attitude. Collectively, we must decide that we want to protect civility and our democratic government. It is our right to receive answers to our questions. Never has this been more important, because we are experiencing new challenges that can have catastrophic consequences for far too many of our fellow citizens.

We must remember that we are all in this together. Suffering does not respect any of our boundaries. Patience and compassion help us calm down and listen to what others have to say. When we take the time to listen to others' perspectives, we can better understand the challenges we all experience. We live now with social distancing and wearing masks. These measures are necessary to reduce the spread of the virus. The additional stress that poor communication creates is unnecessary. Requesting or demanding clear explanations about what is going on should not be viewed as an insult. Instead, it should serve as an opportunity to provide clarity to a suffering population.

I hope that as we continue to navigate the rough seas of COVID-19, we focus on ways to improve the lives of all who suffer. This effort is our responsibility as citizens. Punishing those of us brave enough to expose wrongdoings or genuine emergencies, whether we can successfully address them or not, is intentionally mean and despicable. Let's collectively look forward to opening gates and not erecting them. Speaking truth to power should carry no risk, and without it, civility is what's really at stake.

# Be Truthful

*Being truthful is the new beautiful.*

— Suzy Kassem

⁓

One of the first things our parents teach us is to always tell the truth. We learn that there are consequences for dishonesty. As we grow up, we experience what it feels like when others lie to us. We begin to understand that lying is akin to cheating, which is another dishonorable trait to avoid at all costs. Understanding why we lie and what we can do to change this behavior can bring newfound joy to our lives and the lives of those around us.

Common sense reveals that we lie because we fear the truth or the consequences of speaking the truth. Although this behavior is a wired reaction, it does nothing to help us deal with our daily challenges. Life delivers as many of these challenges as we can handle, and as a result, we experience a feeling of being overwhelmed more often than we'd like.

One area of particular concern is the rumor mill. Rumors, by their very nature, usually lack truth. Part of the mystery around gossip is discovering how much, if any, truth is present. Most of us can recall learning the telephone game when we were in elementary school. We quickly realized how deceptive language can be and how much fun it can be to twist a word or two along the way. By the time the message reached the end of the line, it bore virtually no resemblance to the original message. As we engage in conversations, keep honesty and respect front and center.

Additionally, the cardinal etiquette rule to keep in mind is to refrain from criticizing others when they are not present to defend themselves. Most of us are guilty of engaging in dissing expeditions where we chastise others' faults or indiscretions. This behavior is disrespectful and can be mean spirited. If we find ourselves involved in such conversations, we need to give our heads a shake and consider our motives. Ask yourself, *Who is this benefiting?* The answer will most often be the person who is spewing the gossip, which can degrade someone unable to defend themselves. This commentary is unfortunate, because the goal is for one person to feel better about themselves at someone else's expense. Humility and the Golden Rule come to mind as good self-reflection points for our guilty moments.

In the broader context of life, we depend on our bosses and our civil servants for the truth and to show us, by example, how to handle some of life's most significant challenges. Research has continually revealed that most people in the workforce feel they cannot count on their superiors or coworkers when difficult situations arise. Such lack of support affects productivity as well as the overall culture of an organization. Until organizations successfully address the unnecessary stress this creates, most people will continue to look for a better situation.

In relationships, trust comes with truth. Without trust, relationships wither and die. Our intimate partners and close friends rely on us to always tell the truth. We know how it feels emotionally and physically when someone betrays our trust. The energy required for compassion and forgiveness when someone lies to us can unnecessarily tax our friendships' fragility. One of the most authentic tests of a close relationship is how comfortable we are with sharing uncomfortable truths.

One of the most troubling trends today is that we tend to confuse truth with misinformation, especially when heightened emotions are at the core of the issue. Divisiveness between political parties colors the landscape globally. The result is about half the people believing one thing with complete conviction while the other half think that the opposite is true. Before you decide which side of an issue you agree with, be sure to check on the facts and their sources.

Social media is not a reliable source of truthful information. Instead, the various platforms provide space for people to rant and express emotion-laden opinions. Once we realize that, we can take what we read with a grain of salt. Many of us refrain from interacting on social media, and even more of us refrain from depending on it as a reliable source of news.

White lies are another one of the tools we use when trying to downplay a situation. Although well intentioned, they still skirt the truth. The purpose of a white lie is to protect someone we love from suffering; however, the subject must never be about anything of significance, and honesty may carry an unnecessary sting. As with all lies, the real problem with a white lie is that it often requires more lies to sustain it and can quickly get out of control.

Above all, we have a responsibility as citizens to be truthful in our words and actions. In Don Miguel Ruiz's book *The Four Agreements*, being true to your word is one of the basic tenets by which we should live our lives. In the end, we must be able to depend on ourselves. If we can get up every morning and smile at the face looking back at us in the mirror, life is good.

Remember, honesty is the best policy!

# *Self-Reflective Exercises*

- Do you take responsibility for your actions and your words?

- How much responsibility is enough: part, half, all? My experience suggests that the more responsibility we take for any situation that involves us, the more power we have to make the changes we want to see. Blaming other people or circumstances for our suffering leads only to further suffering.

- How do you take responsibility for your words and actions or the consequences of those words and actions?

- Do you feel awkward when offering an apology? If so, why? What feelings arise when you think about making an apology?

- Do you accept apologies unconditionally? If not, what conditions do you place on others who are apologizing? Do you trust their sincerity? What actions do you take or what words do you use to resolve the suffering at the root of the situation?

# Final Thoughts:
## The Importance of Recognizing Our Strengths and Weaknesses

*Highly sensitive people are too often perceived as weaklings or damaged goods. To feel intensely is not a symptom of weakness; it is the trademark of the truly alive and compassionate. It is not the empath who is broken; society has become dysfunctional and emotionally disabled. There is no shame in expressing your authentic feelings. At times, those described as being a "hot mess" or having "too many issues" are the very fabric of what keeps the dream alive for a more caring, humane world. Never be ashamed to let your tears shine a light in this world.*

— Anthon St. Maarten

We learn the importance of honesty and trust at an early age. These values enrich our lives and, to a large extent, determine the direction our lives will follow. It is essential to surround ourselves with honest and trustworthy people, but we must also practice these values ourselves. Most importantly, we need to check in with ourselves from time to time and rediscover where our strengths and weaknesses reside, look at how they change, and refocus our lives to reflect them. I think an annual checkup is a healthy approach.

Using the six pillars of civility as signposts, we can get a pretty good idea of where we are, where we've been, and where we may want to direct our attention.

Awareness allows us to live mindfully. For some, this can mean delving into one's inner being and uncovering why we enjoy doing the things we enjoy doing. For others, awareness of what and how we experience the world raises our level of engagement and enjoyment in everything we do. Instead of coasting through life bouncing from pillar to post as some people do, we learn to control our lives more quickly by paying more attention to the world around us.

Compassion allows us to accept people as they are without judgment. Self-compassion allows us to accept ourselves as we are, also without judgment. This principle does not encompass approval, condemnation, or forgiveness: it will enable us to simply be our human selves. By removing the need to judge others or ourselves, we can better understand who we are and how we relate to each other. This fundamental understanding helps us choose our friends and decide how much time we want to spend with them.

Humility reminds us that, in essence, we are all equals, a universally understood principle of human rights. How we respect each other is a helpful indicator of how humble we are. In checking our humility barometer, we can see where our prejudices lie as we view others and ourselves. This reflection is critical for overcoming bullying and self-esteem issues. How do we value ourselves and others?

Gratitude is both a state of mind and an action. If we don't express our gratitude, no one will know how much we appreciate what comes our way. For many of us, acknowledging life itself is a daily blessing. Unfortunately, too many of us take so much for granted. Take the time to notice how many of life's simple pleasures you find around you. Being grateful for our friends, our health, and our many skills can be very grounding. It can be a real eye-opener, too. The bonus about gratitude is that our lives become open to even greater abundance when we express it. Noticing the presence of this dynamic in our lives is a great stress reliever, too.

Encouragement is the elixir that we all need to keep going with confidence and a good sense of purpose. Establishing trust and healthy relationships and making our connections with others have real meaning require us to encourage one another. Encouragement can take the form of a reward: a bonus, raise at work, or praise. Everyone benefits from encouragement because it is a kind and loving way to connect, the keystone of living.

Responsibility is a moral obligation and duty that we all need to be aware of. Taking responsibility for the good things in our life is easy. When we face challenges, however, we sometimes revert to blaming life's mishaps on others. We pawn off our responsibility instead of owning it. The reverse is also true. How often do we nose our way into other people's lives and decision-making processes when the outcome is none of our business? This dynamic is not uncommon within families or in our relationships with close friends and business associates. It's helpful to take responsibility for our feelings during stressful times as much as possible. We alone have the power and ability to change how we feel about something. We must also remember to allow others the same opportunity.

I hope you score high marks as you look at these signposts along your life path. By looking at them, we can begin to understand where we need to adjust. These adjustments lead us to a more fulfilling life, something that is a right for which we can all be grateful.

# *In Gratitude*

After completing the first draft of this book, I realized how many people assisted me during its gestation. I wrote the essays that inspired it over a decade. They appeared initially as newspaper columns in the *Telegraph Journal*, a regional eastern Canadian publication. I thank them—Jamie Irving in particular—for trusting me and paying me over the years to write about my passion: etiquette and civility.

Out of the kindness of her heart, Liz Wold encouraged me through many of these years with her editorial advice, helping me become a clearer communicator.

Every day, as a recovering alcoholic, I thank three women who, by their example, encouragement, and kindness, helped save me from a far different life: Missy Lickle, Sophie Craighead, and Pamela Eyring.

My therapist, Liz Neve, is one of the most insightful people I have ever met. She opened my eyes to trauma-induced suffering. Without this, I would very likely have missed connecting our declining civility to our traumatized society with hope for healing and recovery. Liz introduced me to the magnitude of compassion, especially self-compassion. Her consistent encouragement supported this "little engine that could."

I am grateful to my sister, Elizabeth Kipp, an author and mentor to many struggling with chronic pain, who shared not only her insights but also her editor, Robyn Fritz, whose gentle counsel guided me through the "this makes no sense" moments of editing. Elizabeth shared the importance of being grateful for just about everything life throws at us.

Of *Society Texas* fame, Lance Morgan and Rob Giardinelli stoked the flames to complete this book with a keen eye to detail, many helpful suggestions, and unrelenting encouragement.

I wish there were grander words than "thank you" for expressing my gratitude to Greg Cohane, who designed the beautiful book cover. Over the years, he has also helped me to be more aware of others' feelings. I also thank Robert Lanphear, who handled layout and design, and Laurel Robinson for her exquisite copyediting.

Life teems with serendipity. Meeting one of my mentors, Andy Faas, has helped me understand the connectivity of the many characteristics of leadership. His honest and forthright approach to governance on many levels reveals the need for significant reform as a return to civility.

Sharon Schweitzer has encouraged me through much of this process, giving me the confidence to appreciate that what I do has value.

William Hanson, Britain's most sparkling etiquette expert, has been a constant source of amusement and validation on all points of etiquette. His foreword in this book reflects our mutual appreciation for each other's work.

# *About Jay*

Jay's mission is to help alleviate as much suffering as possible that so many people endure. Through his hundreds of newspaper columns and television broadcasts across Canada on CHCO-TV as Canada's Etiquette Guy, he has explained and encouraged good manners and civil behavior as a way to de-stress and learn to embrace and enjoy our complex lives.

Jay's interest in self-discovery began in the 1970s when he studied with a variety of spiritual teachers, therapists, and healers. As he formed stronger connections with both his inner wisdom and higher power, he began to uncover and heal from unresolved childhood traumas. His journey of dedicated work enables him to share with others the value of living a balanced life in a chaotic world and how to create one.

Since emigrating to Canada in 1995 from New York City, Jay has been the catalyst for numerous individuals and organizations to regain control during challenging times. He successfully mentors people who are committed to discovering the miracles that lie within them through one-on-one discussions and self-reflective exercises. *The 6 Pillars of Civility* is the template he created as the foundation for his work.

Full podcasts of many of the newspaper columns upon which this work is based are available at https://www.facebook.com/LemonadeMentoring.

Jay lives in Saint Andrews, New Brunswick, Canada.

Manufactured by Amazon.ca
Bolton, ON